POP STANDARDS
FOR ACCORDION

ISBN 978-1-5400-1448-1

7777 W. Bluemound Rd. P.O. Box 13819 Milwaukee, WI 53213

Visit Hal Leonard Online at
www.halleonard.com

ALL MY LOVING

Words and Music by JOHN LENNON
and PAUL McCARTNEY

1.
2., 3.
C7
F
E♭7
D7
A7
loving to you. 2. I'll pre-
All my
Dm
A7
F
loving
I will send to
you.
To Coda
A7
Dm
A7
F
All my
loving,
darling, I'll be
true.
Interlude
B♭
F

Gm
C7
F
3
3
m
7
M

D
D.S. al Coda
Close your

CODA
F
C/E
true.
All my
M

Dm
F
lov - ing,
all
my
lov- ing,
ooh,
all
my
m
M

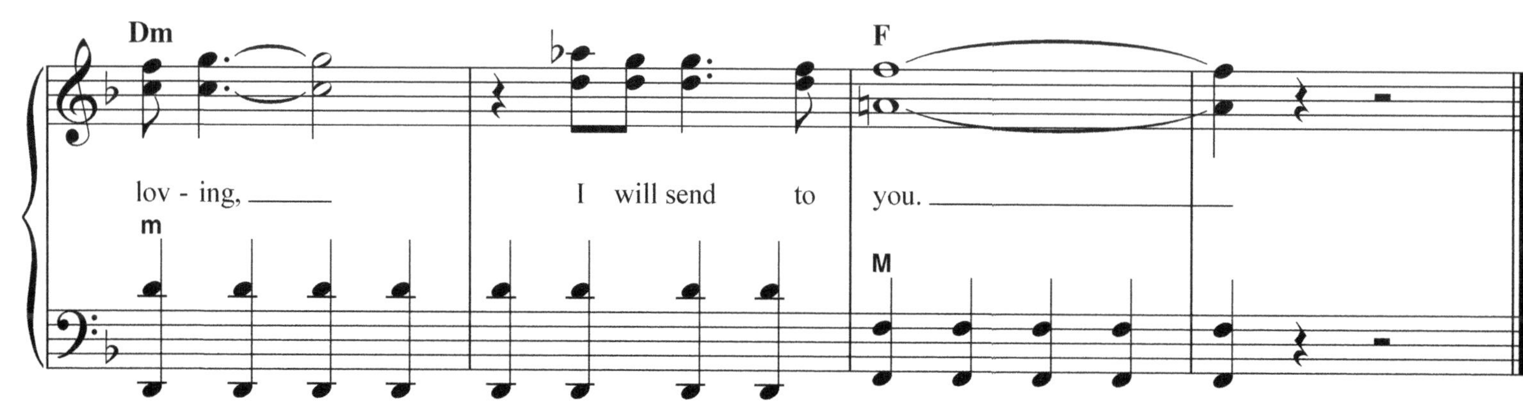
Dm
F
lov - ing,
I will send
to
you.
m
M

ANNIE'S SONG

Words and Music by
JOHN DENVER

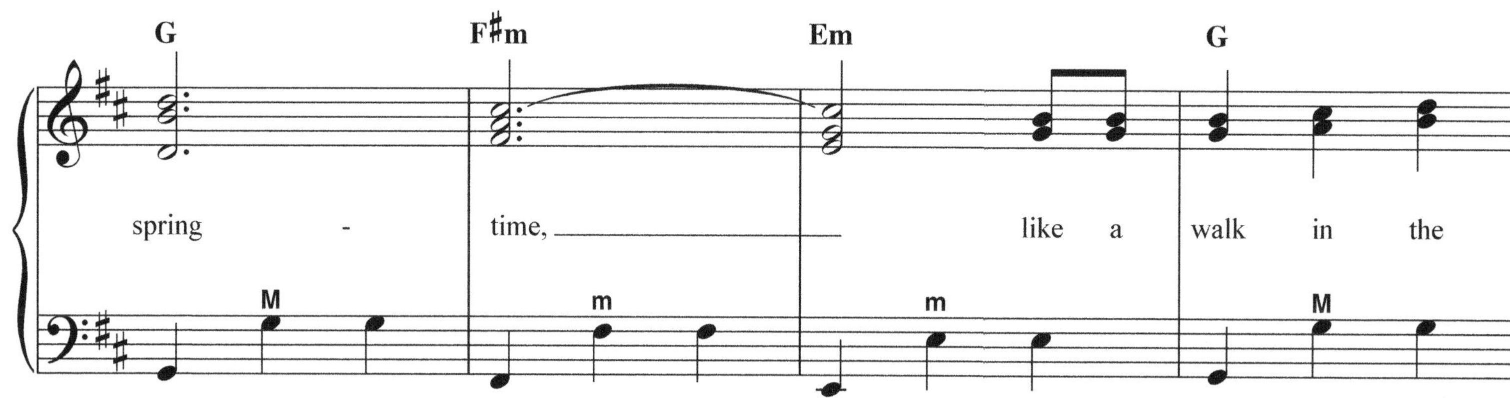
G
F♯m
Em
G
spring - time, like a walk in the
M
m
m
M

A7
rain, like a storm in the
7

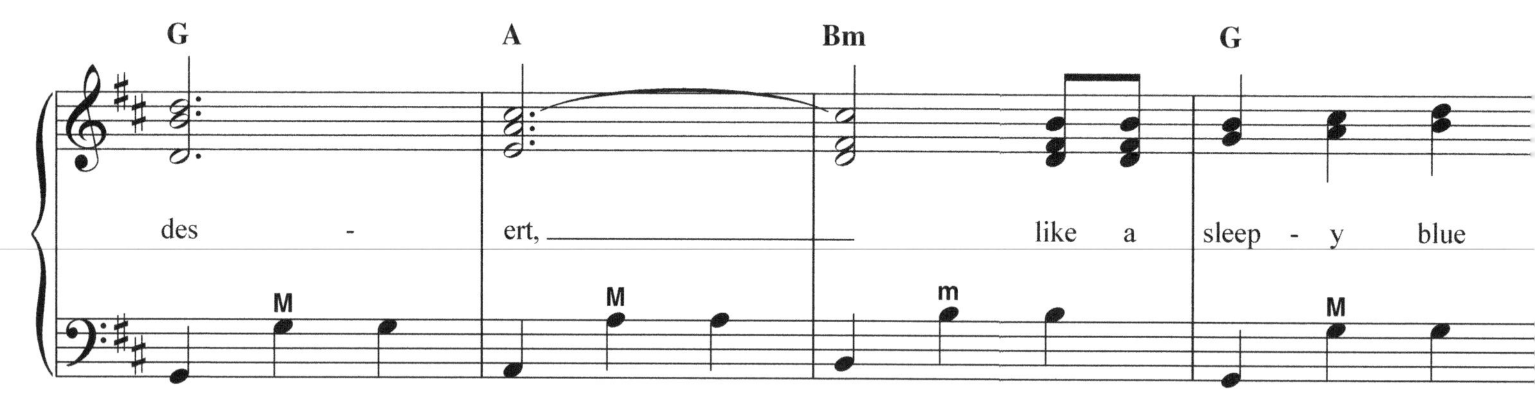
G
A
Bm
G
des - ert, like a sleep - y blue
M
M
m
M

D
o - cean. You fill up my
M

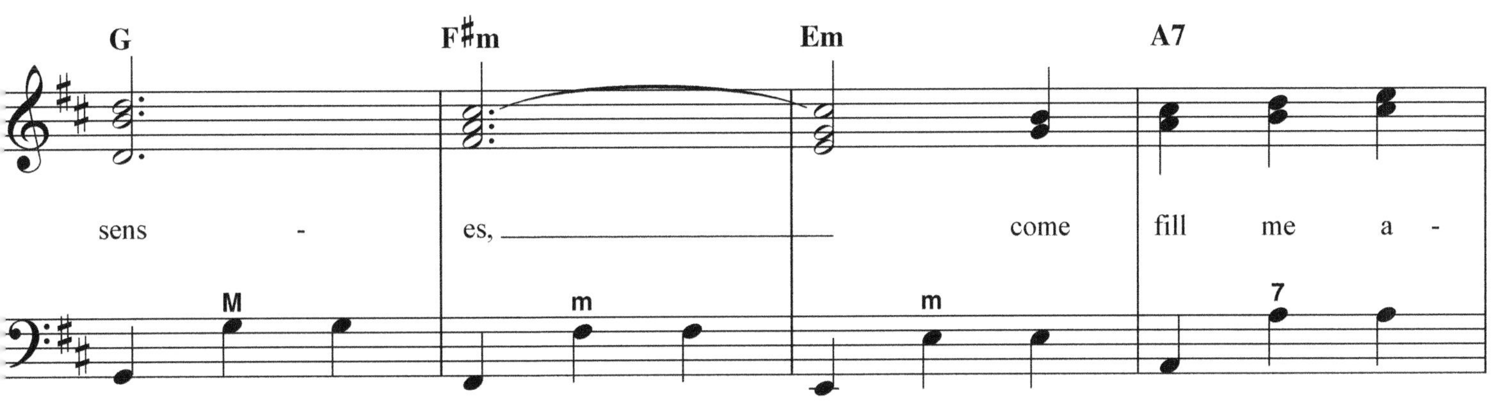
G
F♯m
Em
A7
sens - es, come fill me a -
M
m
m
7

D
G/D
D
gain.
Come let me
M
M
M

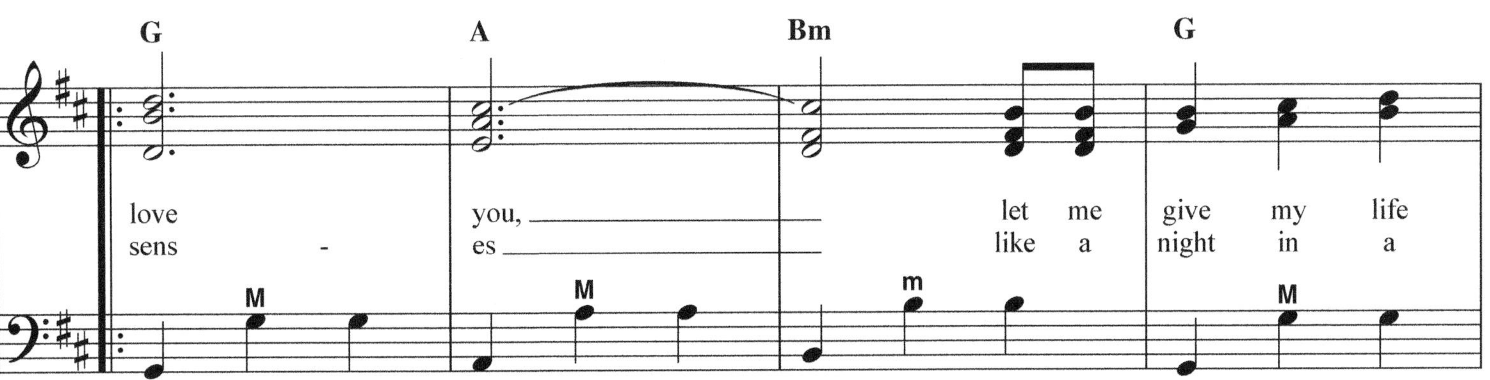
G
A
Bm
G
love you, let me give my life
sens - es like a night in a
M
M
m
M

D
to you, let me drown in your
for - est, like the moun - tains in
M

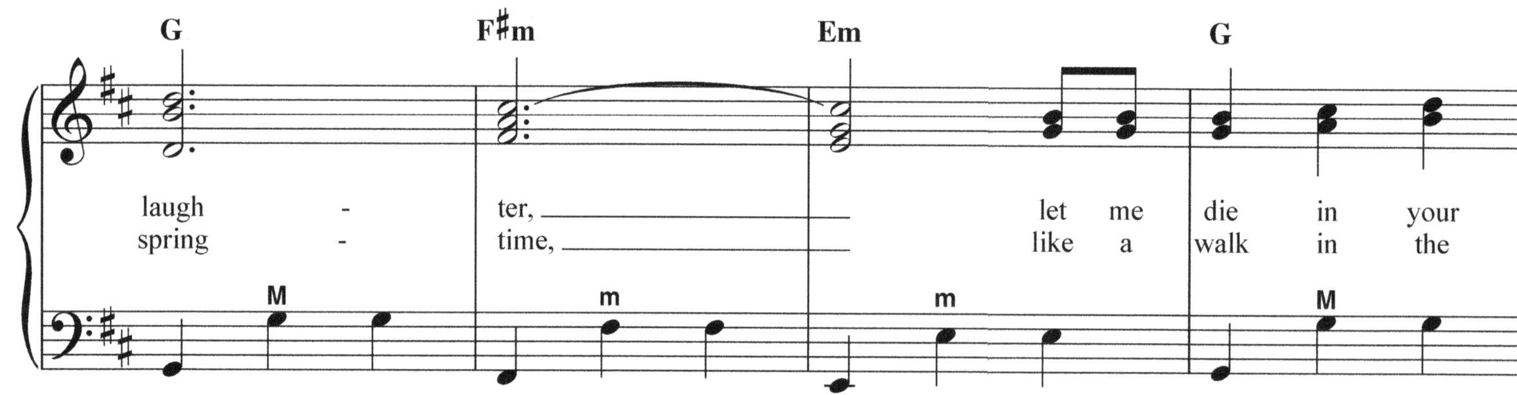
G F♯m Em G
laugh - ter, let me die in your
spring - time, like a walk in the
M m m M

A7
arms. Let me lay down be -
rain, like a storm in the
7

G A Bm G
side you, let me al - ways be
des - ert, like a sleep - y blue
M M m M

D
with you. Come let me
o - cean. You fill up my
M

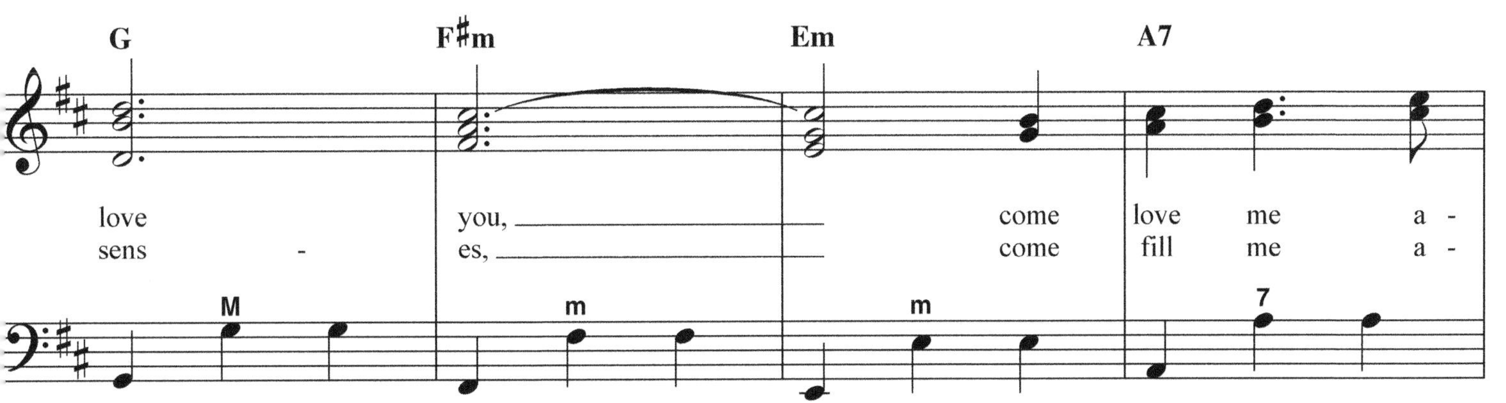
G
F♯m
Em
A7
love
you,
come
love
me
a -
sens -
es,
come
fill
me
a -
M
m
m
7

1.
D
G/D
D
gain.
You
fill
up
my
M
M
M

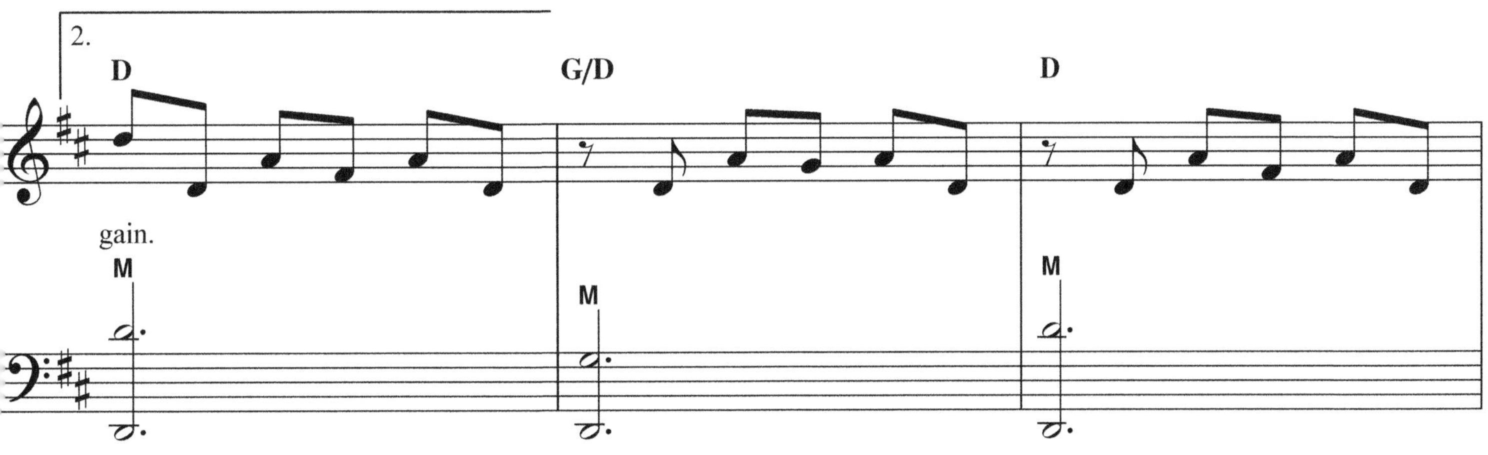
2.
D
G/D
D
gain.
M
M
M

Em/D
D
G/D
D
m
M
M
M

CAN'T SMILE WITHOUT YOU

Words and Music by CHRIS ARNOLD,
DAVID MARTIN and GEOFF MORROW

G
Em
feel sad when you're sad. I feel glad when
M
m

Am
3
you're glad, if you ___ on - ly knew what I'm ___ go - ing through;
m

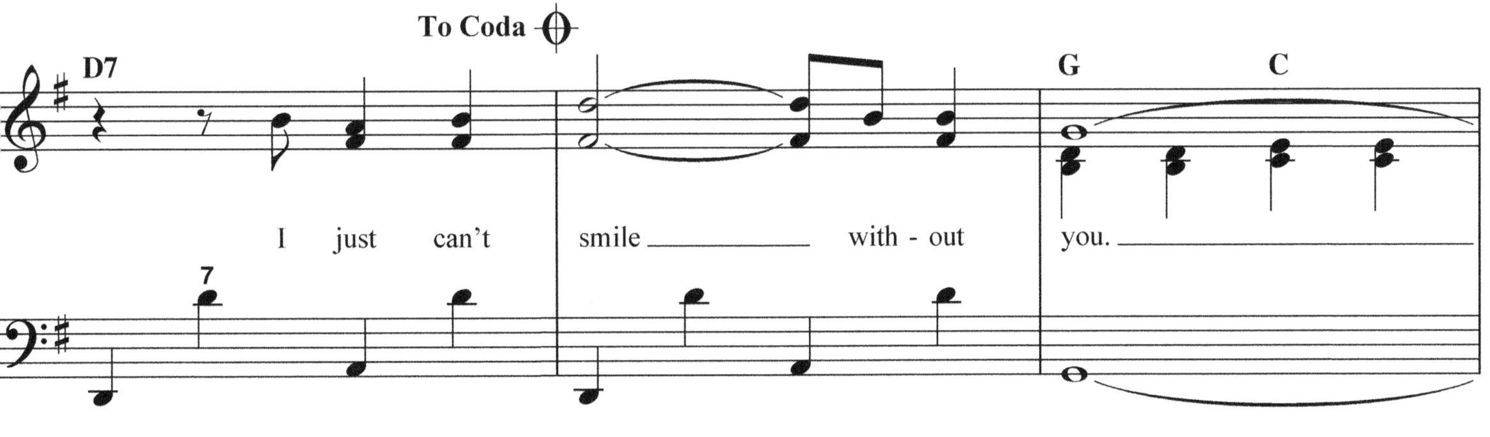
To Coda
D7
G C
I just can't smile ___ with - out you. ___
7

G C
G
Em
___ You came a - long ___ just like a song ___ and
M
m

Am
D7
G
3
bright-ened my day.
Who'd-a be-lieved that you were
part of a dream?
m
7
M

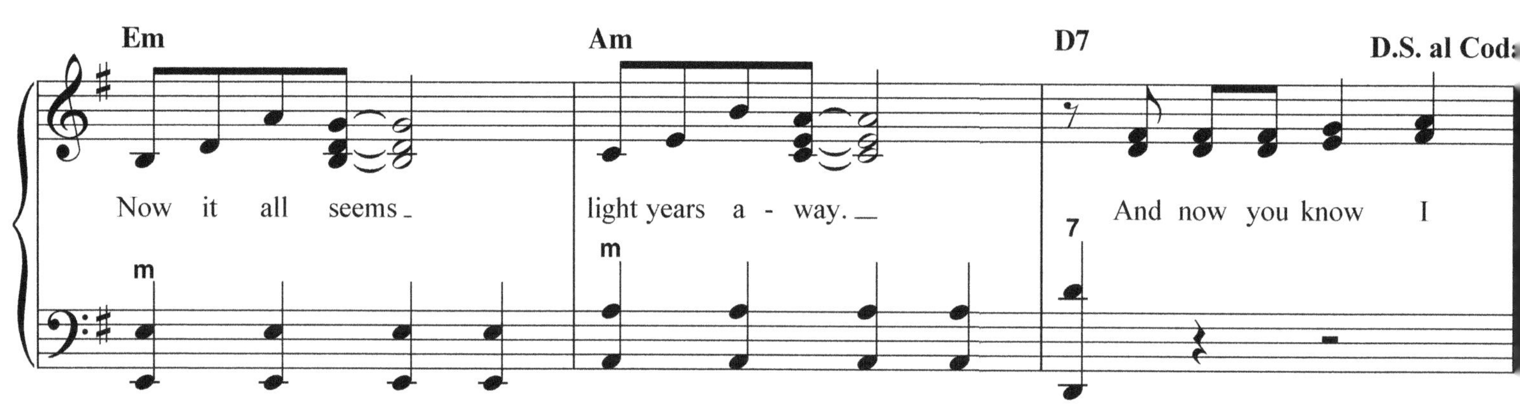
Em
Am
D7
D.S. al Coda
Now it all seems
light years a - way.
And now you know I
m
m
7

CODA
Am
D7
Dm
smile.
Now,
some peo - ple say
hap - pi - ness takes
m
7
m

G7
C
Cm
so ver - y long to
find.
Well, I'm
find - ing it hard
7
M
m

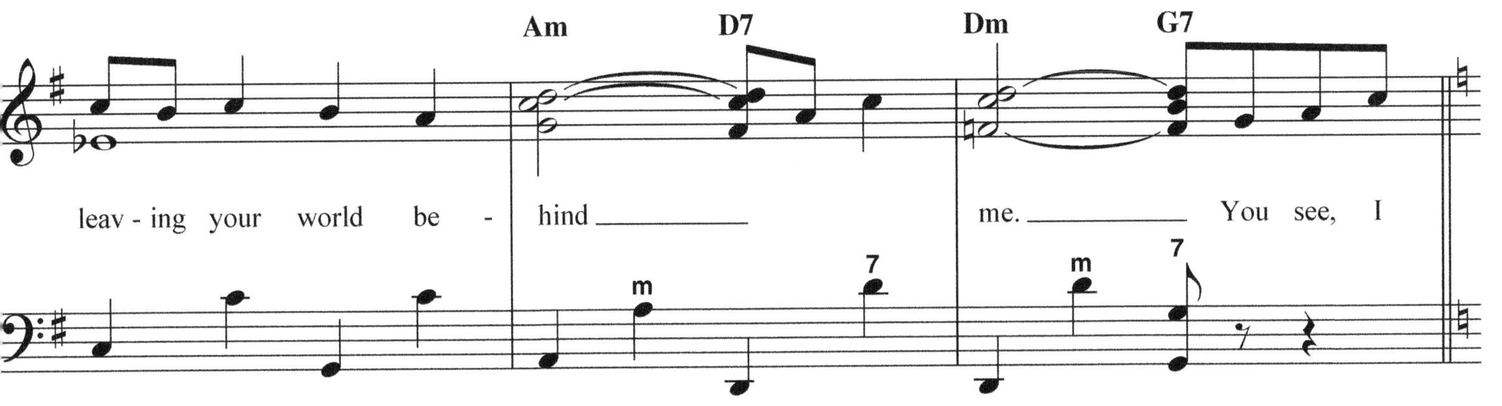
Am
D7
Dm
G7
leav - ing your world be - hind
me.
You see, I
m
7
m
7

C
Am
can't smile with - out you.
I can't smile with - out you. If
M
m

Dm
G7
you on - ly knew what I'm go - ing through;
I just can't
3
3
m
7

C
smile with-out you.

CHANCES ARE

Words by AL STILLMAN
Music by ROBERT ALLEN

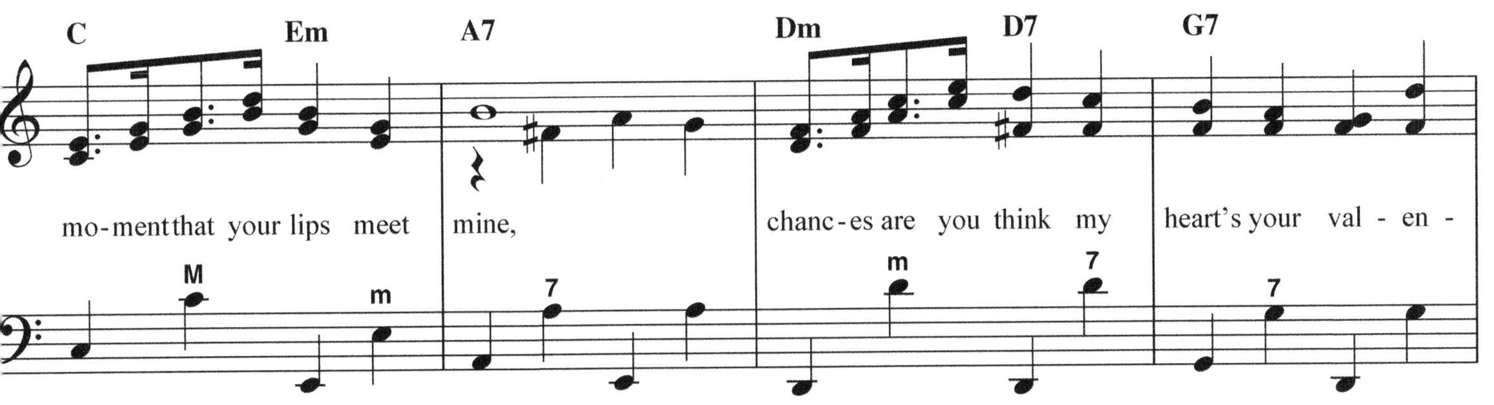
C
Em
A7
Dm
D7
G7
mo-ment that your lips meet mine,
chanc-es are you think my heart's your val - en -
M
m
7
m
7
7

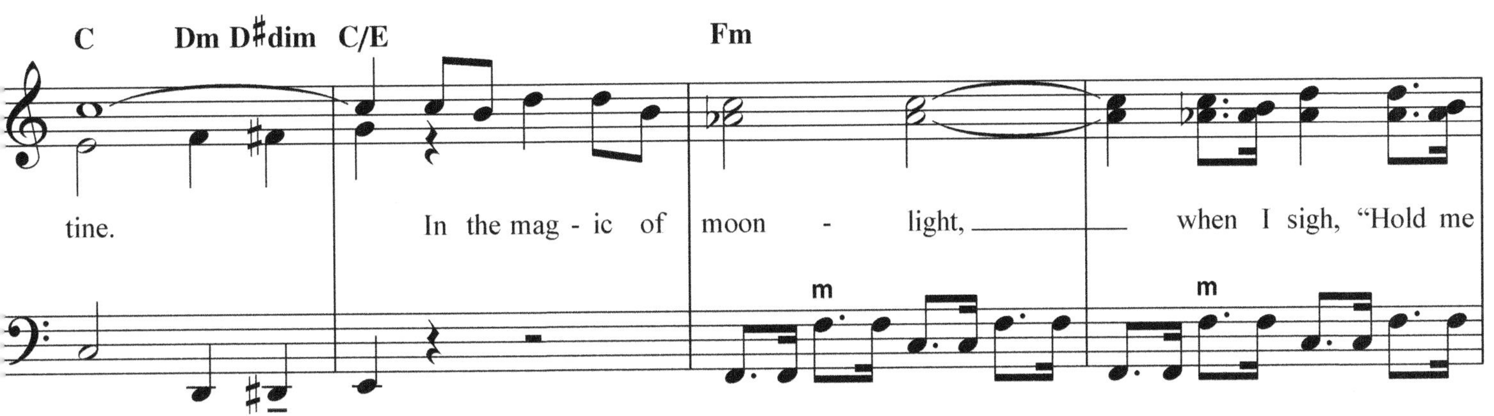
C
Dm D♯dim
C/E
Fm
tine.
In the mag - ic of moon - light,
when I sigh, "Hold me
m
m

Cm
Cm/A
close, dear,"
chanc - es are you be - lieve the stars that
m
m

D7
A♭7
G7
C7
fill the skies, are in my eyes.
Guess you feel you'll al - ways
7
7

F
Fm/D
C
Em
be the one and on - ly one for me. And if you think you could,
M
m
M
m

A7
Dm
C/E
F
F♯dim
1.
G7
C
G7
well, chanc - es are your chanc - es are aw - f'ly good.
7
7
M
7

C
C7
2.
G7
Gm/E
A7
Chanc - es are aw - f'ly good; the chanc - es
M
7
7
m
7

Dm
G7
C
A♭/C
C
are your chanc - es are aw - f'ly good.
m
7
M

FOR ONCE IN MY LIFE

Words by RONALD MILLER
Music by ORLANDO MURDEN

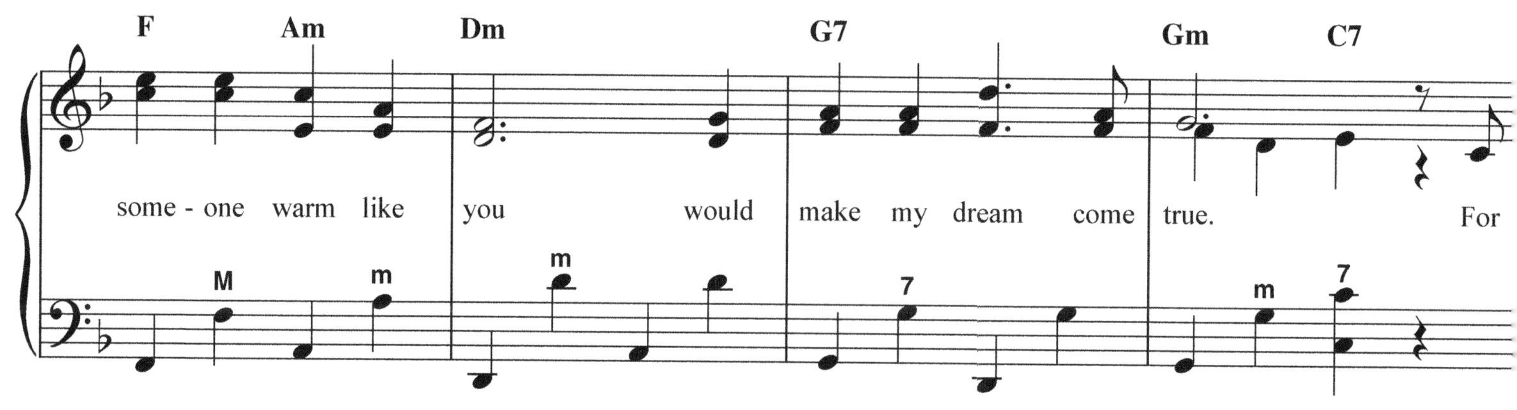
F
Am
Dm
G7
Gm
C7
some - one warm like you would make my dream come true. For
M
m
m
7
m
7

F
Cdim/F♯
Gm
E♭/G
C7
D7
once in my life I won't let sor-row hurt me, not like it's hurt me be - fore. For
M
dim
m
M
7

Gm
E♭/G
C7
F
C7/G
F/A
once I have some-thing I know won't de-sert me, I'm not a - lone an - y - more. For
m
M
7
M
7
M

Dm
Dm/C♯
Dm/C
Dm/B
B♭
G7/B
once I can say this is mine, you can't take it, long as I know I have love, I can make it. For
M
7

1.
F
B♭
F/A
Gm
C7
F
Dm
once in my life I have some - one who needs me.
M
M
m
Gm
C7
2.
F
Gm
C7
C♯dim
For once I can feel that some - bod - y's heard my
m
7
M
m
Dm
G7
F
plea.
For once in my life I have
m
7
M
B♭
F/A
Gm
C7
Dm/B
B♭m
F/A
A♭dim
Gm
G♭
F
some - one who needs me.

HELP ME MAKE IT THROUGH THE NIGHT

Words and Music by
KRIS KRISTOFFERSON

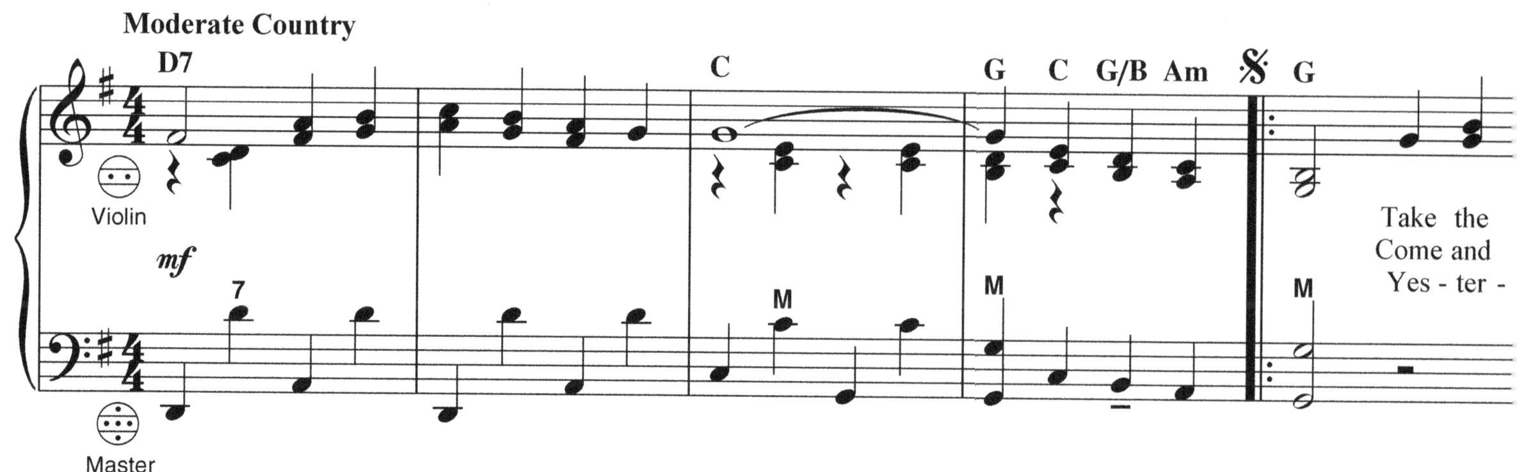

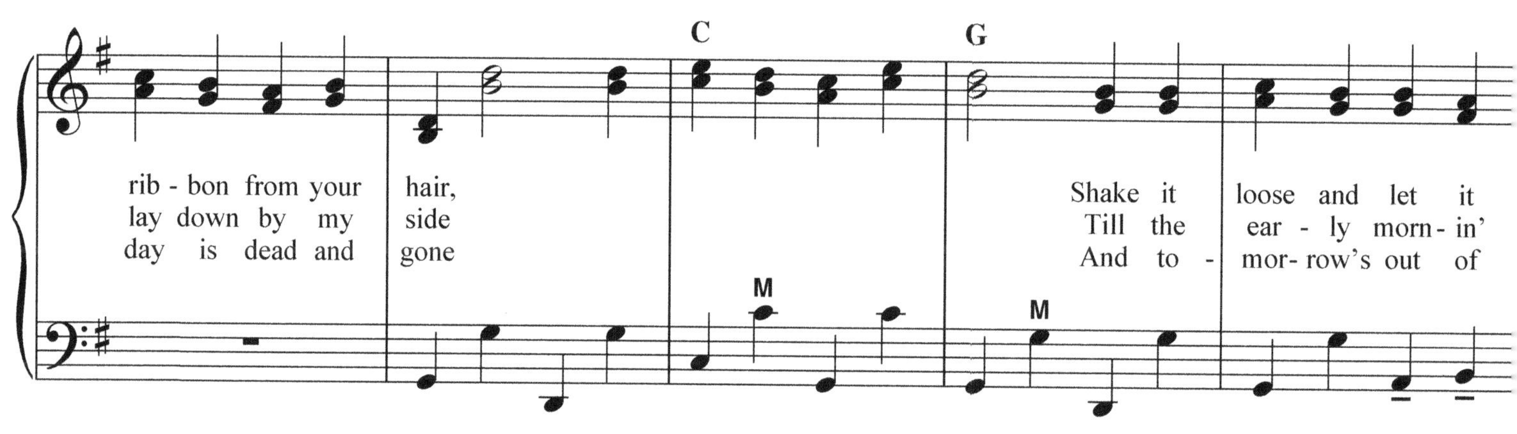

To Coda
1.
G
Like the shad - ows on the wall.
M
C G/B Am
2.
G
Help me make it through the night.
M
C
G
C
I don't care who's right or wrong.
M
M
M
G
I don't try to un - der - stand.
M

3
A7
Let the dev - il take to - mor - row.
7

3
D7
Lord, to - night I need a friend.
7

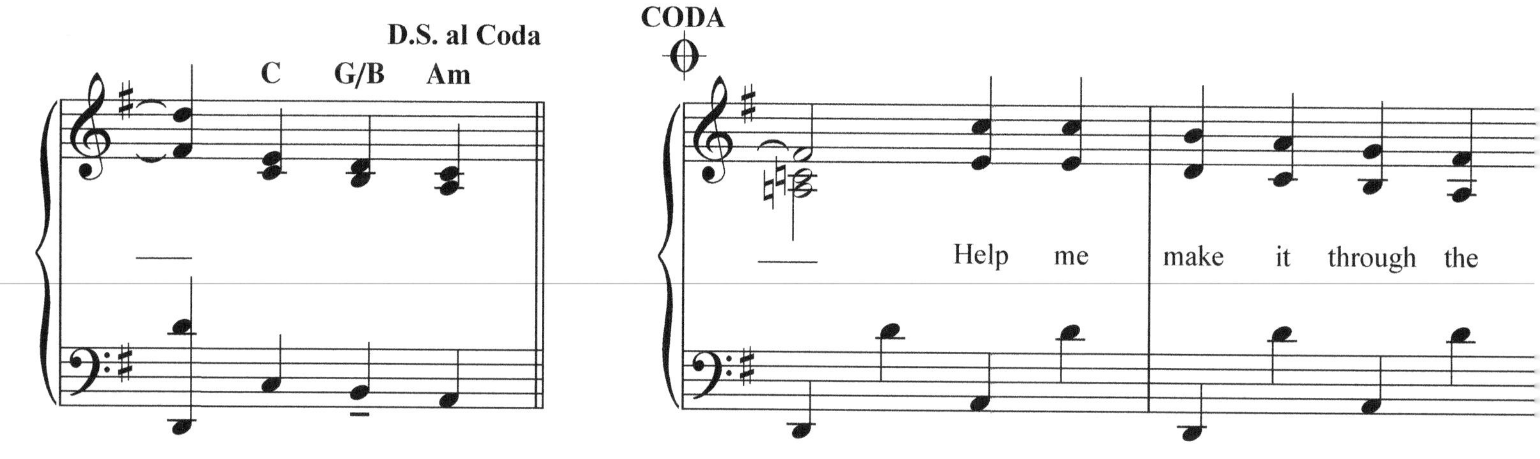
D.S. al Coda
C G/B Am
CODA
Help me make it through the

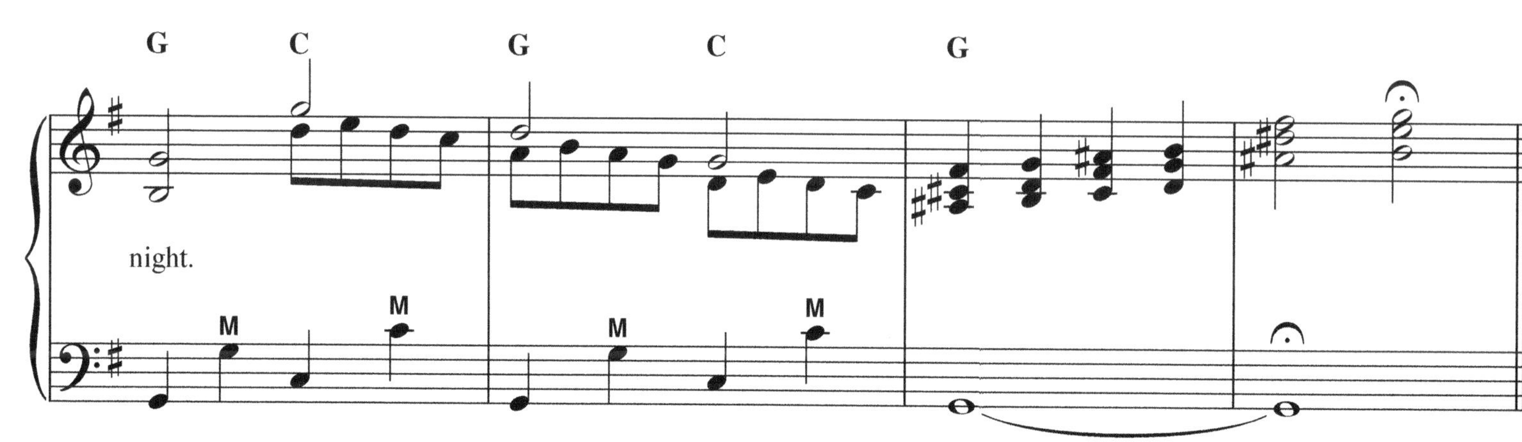
G C G C G
night.
M M M M

MY CHERIE AMOUR

Words and Music by STEVIE WONDER,
SYLVIA MOY and HENRY COSBY

D7
G
C7
my Che - rie A - mour,
I've been near you but you
may - be some - day I'll
dis - tant as the Milk - y
nev - er no - ticed
share your lit - tle dis - tant
F
D7
C
Way.
me.
cloud.
My Che - rie A - mour,
My Che - rie A - mour,
My Che - rie A - mour,
D7
F7
E7
pret - ty lit - tle one that I a - dore,
won't you tell me how could you ig - nore
pret - ty lit - tle one that I a - dore,
you're the on - ly girl my
that be - hind that lit - tle
you're the on - ly girl my
A7
D7
To Coda
1.
G
heart beats for;
smile I wore,
heart beats for;
how I wish that you were
mine.

2.
D7
G
D7
In a
mine.
La la
7
M
7
D.S. al Coda
C
F
D7
G
D7
la la ___ la
la, la la
la la ___ la
la. May - be
7
CODA
G
F7
G
D7
C
mine. ___
La la
la la ___ la
7
F
F7
1.
G
D7
2.
G
la, la la
la la ___ la
la. La la
la.
7

QUIET VILLAGE

By LES BAXTER

1.
2.
E/F
F
B♭/C
F
me.
me.
A -
A -
M

Cm
F7
Cm
bove me,
there's a moon on
fire,
m
7
m

F7
B♭
3
telling you to
love me
as I de -
7
M

B♭m
C7
G♭7
F
sire.
And ev - er the
flame
m
7
M

D7
Gm
C
D7
in my qui - et
vil - lage will burn,
dar - ling till the
7
m
M
7

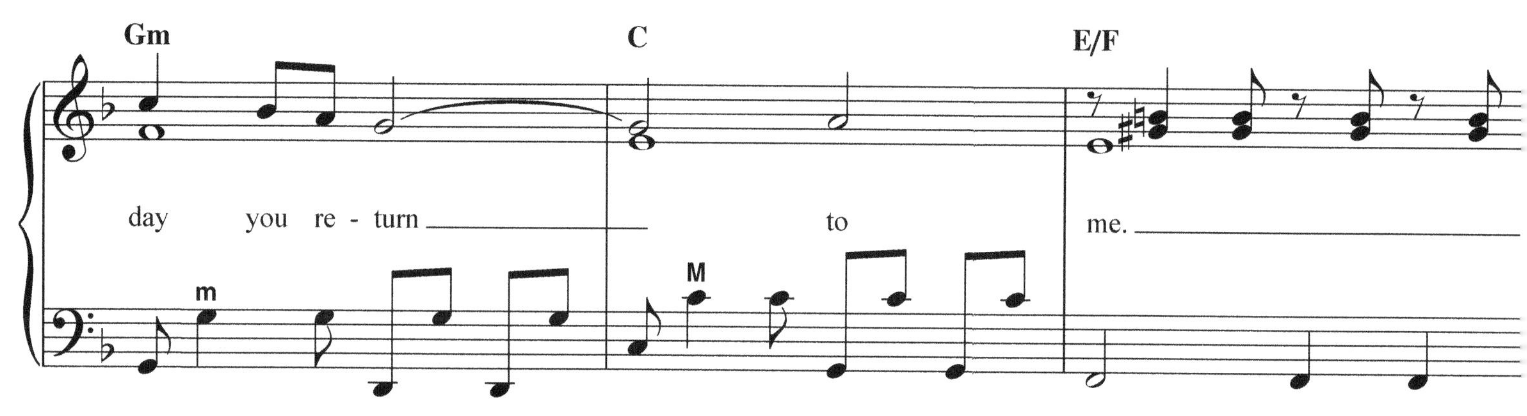
Gm
C
E/F
day you re - turn
to
me.
m
M

F
B♭/C
E/F
F
B♭/C
3
3
Re - turn to
me,
re - turn to
M
M

F
A♭/G♭
F
me.

QUE SERA, SERA
(Whatever Will Be, Will Be)

Words and Music by JAY LIVINGSTON
and RAYMOND B. EVANS

Bb
F
ra, se - ra,
what - ev - er will be will be.
M
M

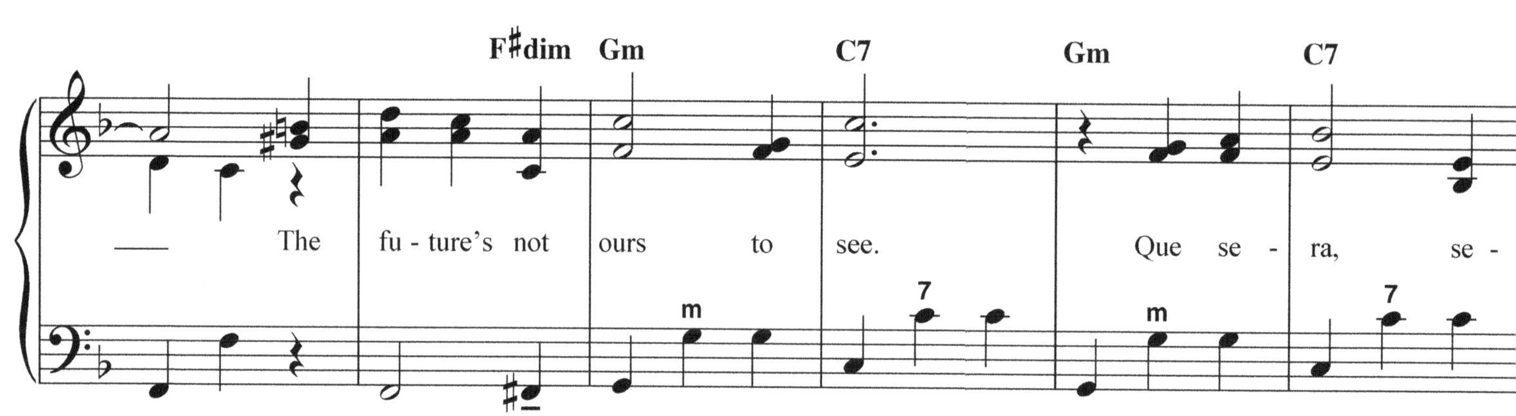
F#dim Gm C7 Gm C7
The fu - ture's not ours to see. Que se - ra, se -
m
7
m
7

F Gm C7 F
To Coda
ra:
What will be will be!"
M
m
7
M

1.
C7
2., 3.
C7 F
When I was
When I grew up and fell in
Now I have chil - dren of my
M

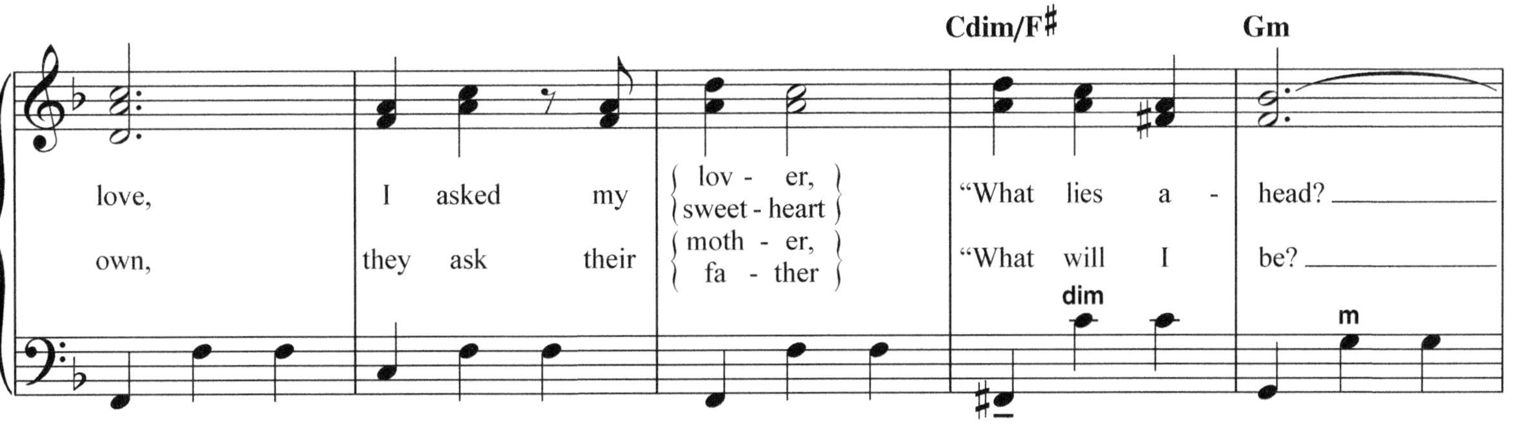
Cdim/F♯
Gm
love,
I asked my
lov - er,
sweet - heart
"What lies a - head?
own,
they ask their
moth - er,
fa - ther
"What will I be?
dim
m

C7
Will we have
rain - bows
day af - ter
day?"
Will I be
pret - ty?
hand - some
Will I be
rich?"
7

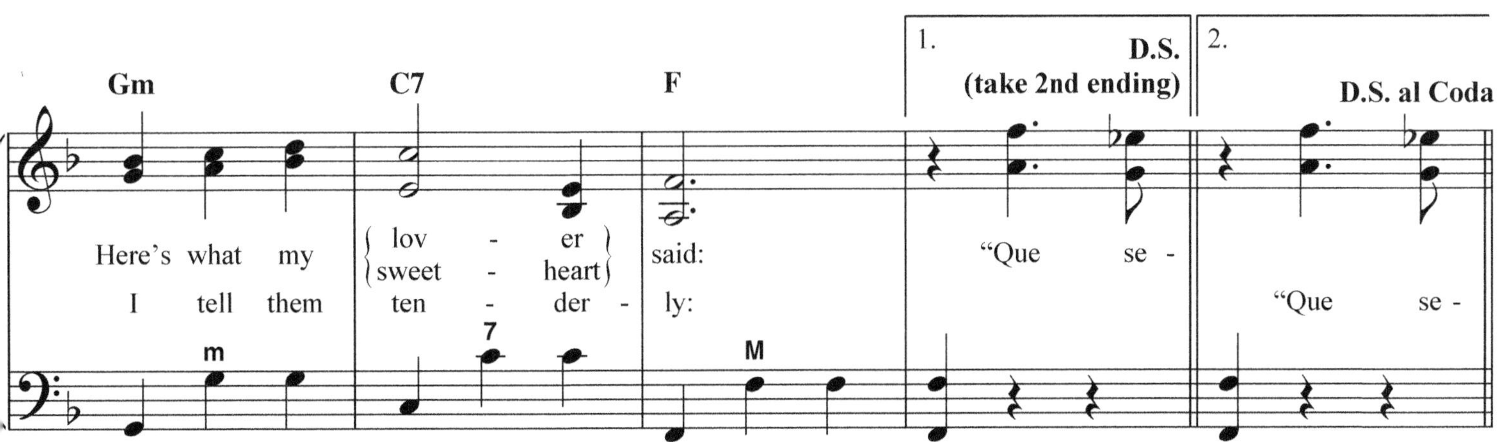
Gm
C7
F
1.
D.S.
(take 2nd ending)
2.
D.S. al Coda
Here's what my
lov - er
sweet - heart
said:
"Que se -
I tell them
ten - der - ly:
"Que se -
m
7
M

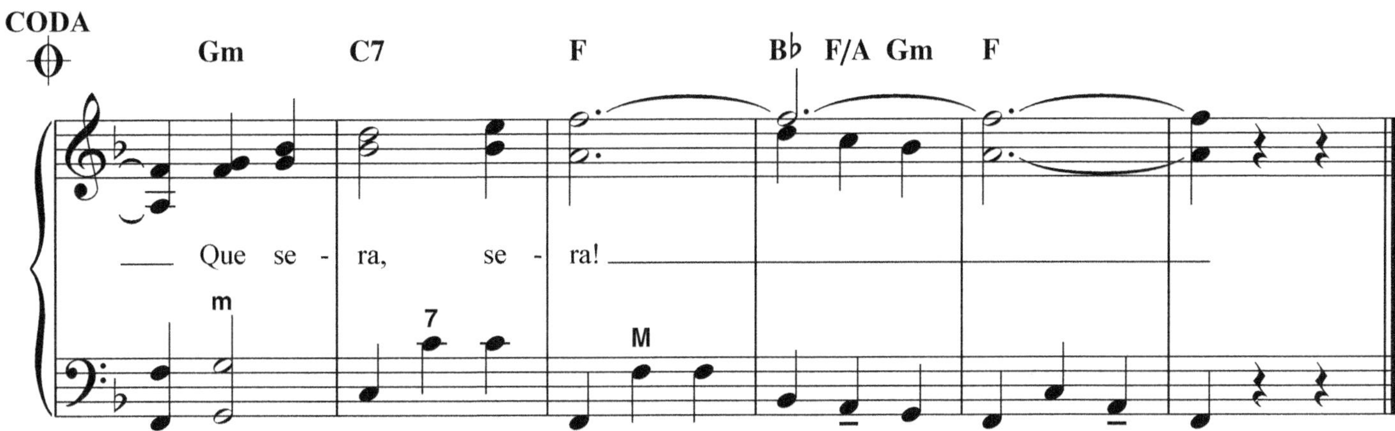
CODA
Gm
C7
F
B♭
F/A
Gm
F
Que se - ra, se - ra!
m
7
M

RAMBLIN' ROSE

Words and Music by NOEL SHERMAN
and JOE SHERMAN

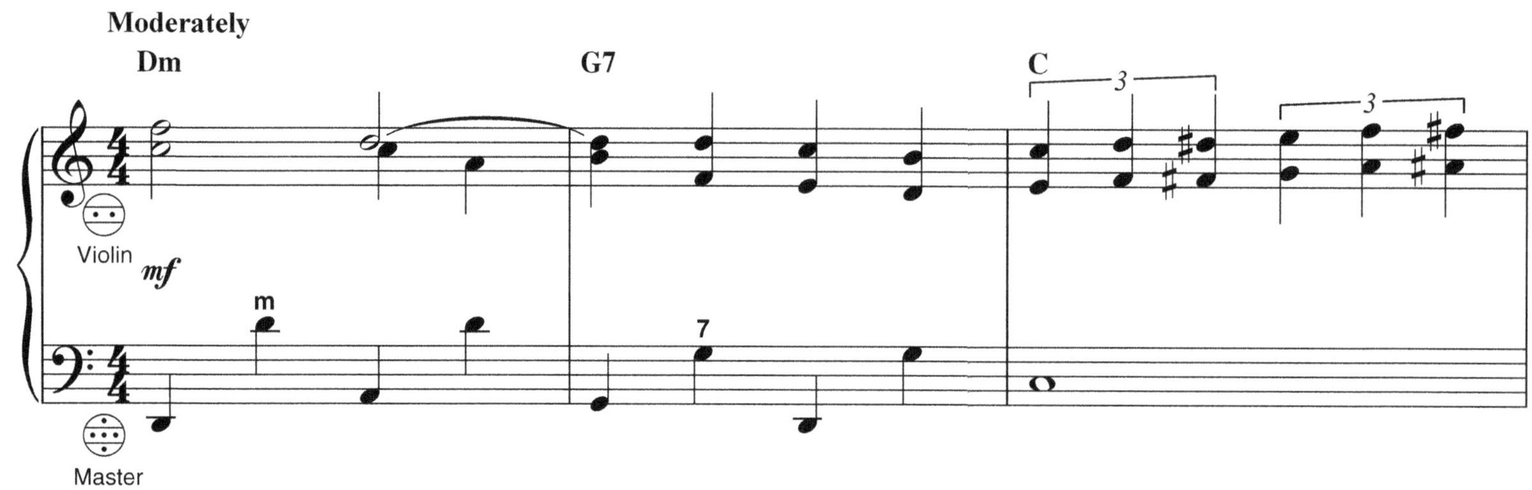

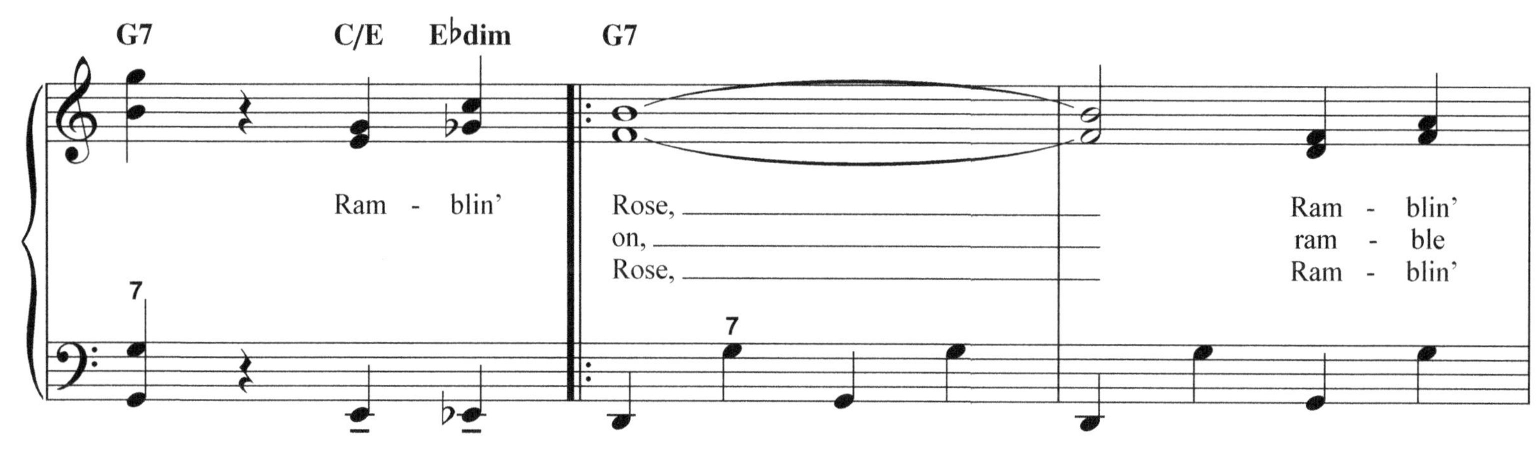

G7
C7
no one knows. Wild and
days are gone, who will
heav - en knows. Though I
7
7

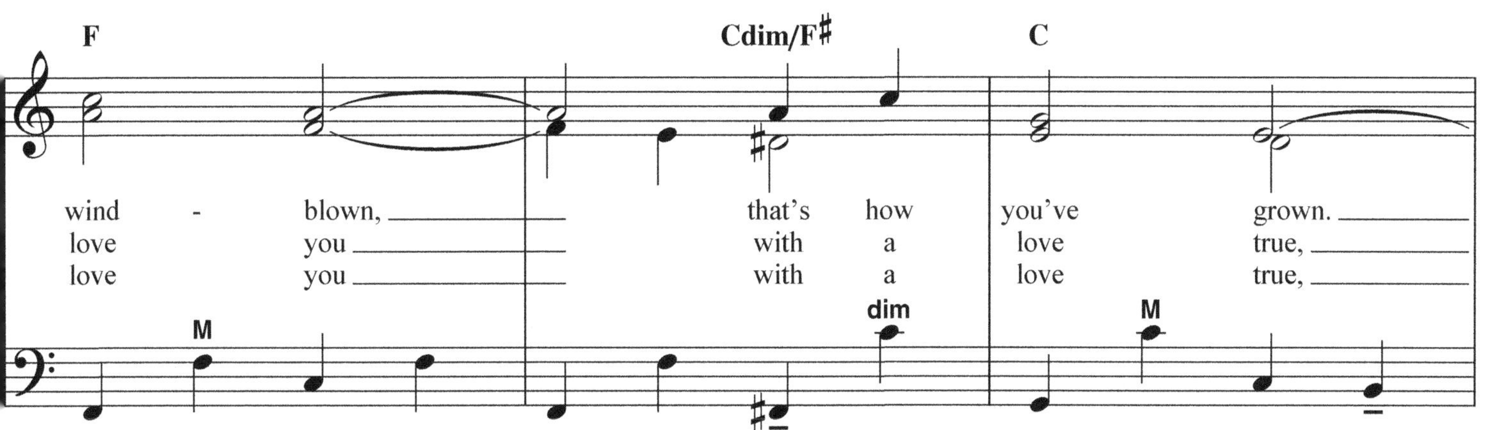
F
Cdim/F♯
C
wind - blown, that's how you've grown.
love you with a love true,
love you with a love true,
M
dim
M

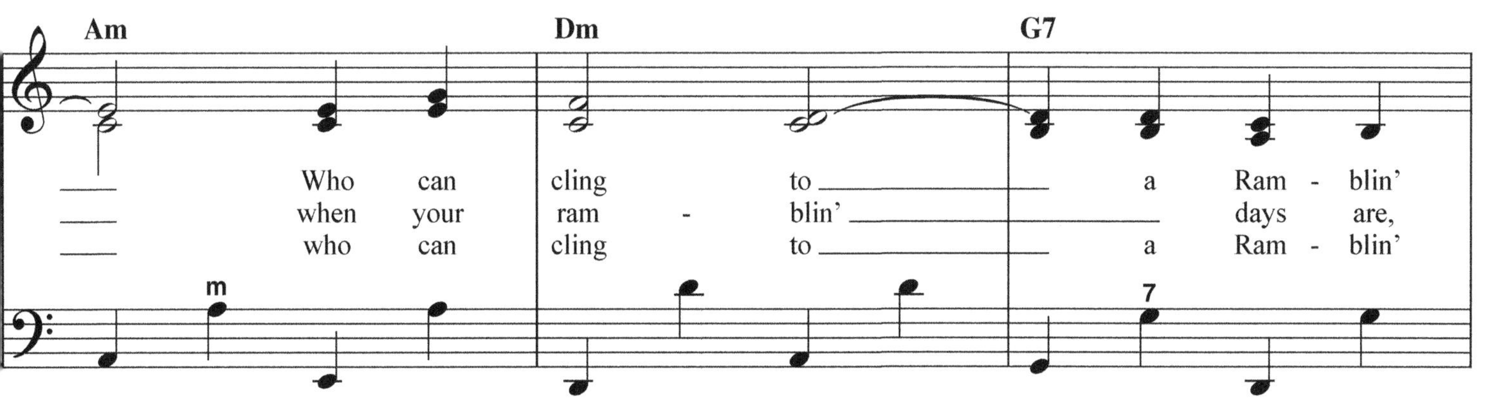
Am
Dm
G7
Who can cling to a Ram - blin'
when your ram - blin' days are,
who can cling to a Ram - blin'
m
7

1., 2.
C
F
C
C/E
E♭dim
3.
C
Rose? Ram - ble
gone? Ram - blin'
Rose?
M
M
M

(Sittin' On)
THE DOCK OF THE BAY

Words and Music by STEVE CROPPER
and OTIS REDDING

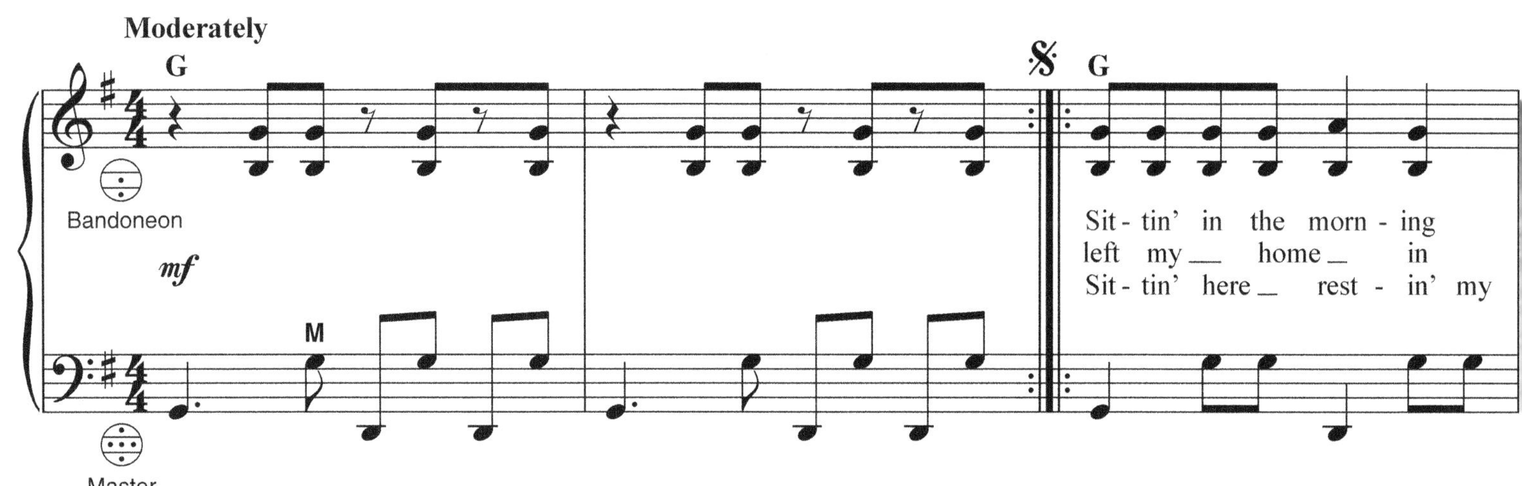

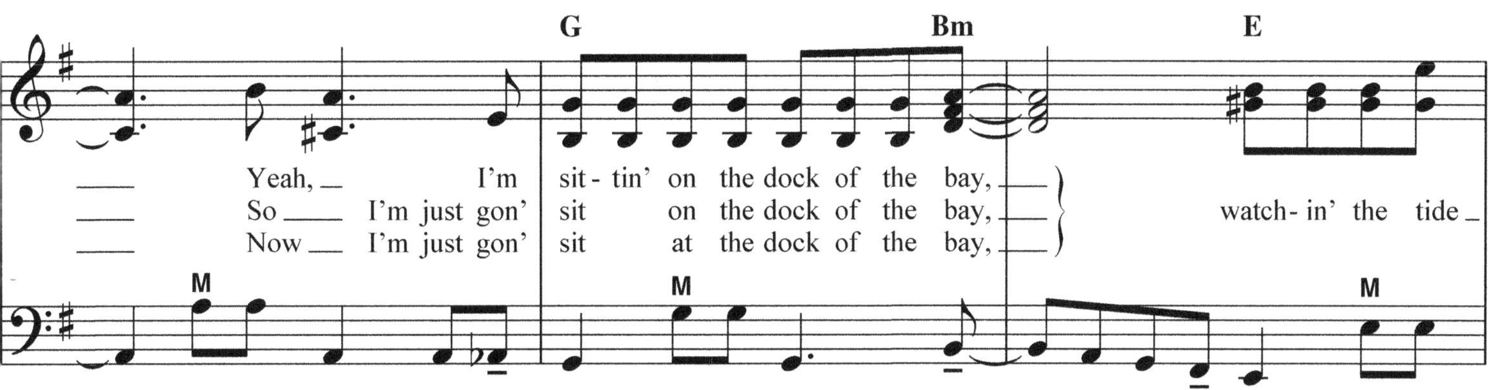
G
Bm
E
Yeah, I'm sit - tin' on the dock of the bay,
So I'm just gon' sit on the dock of the bay,
Now I'm just gon' sit at the dock of the bay,
watch - in' the tide
M
M
M

G
Bm
E
G
A
roll a - way. Ooh, I'm just sit - tin' on the dock of the bay,
M
M
M

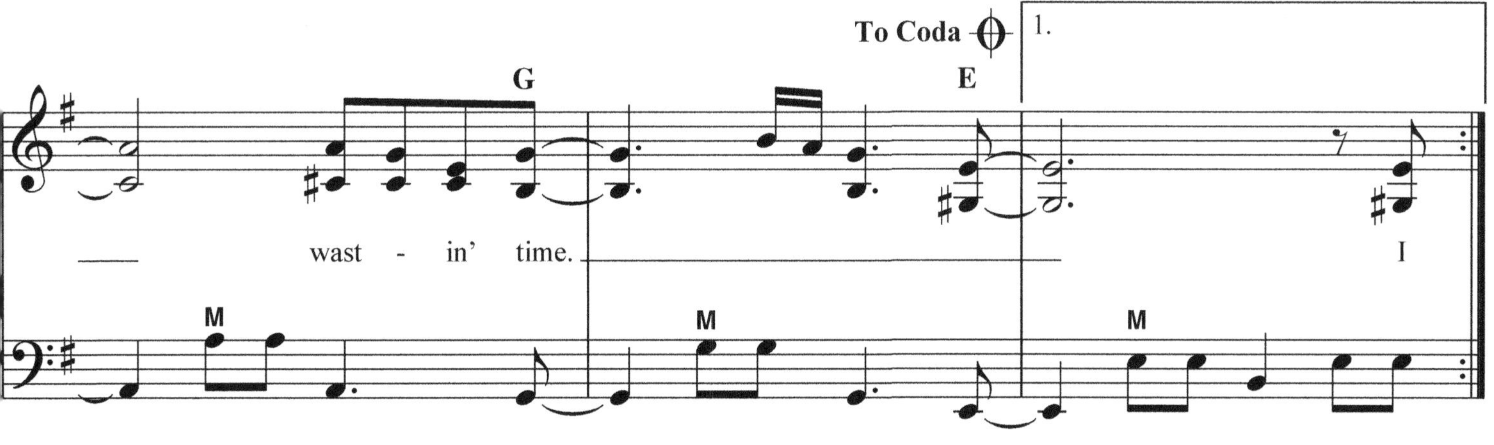
To Coda
1.
G
E
wast - in' time. I
M
M
M

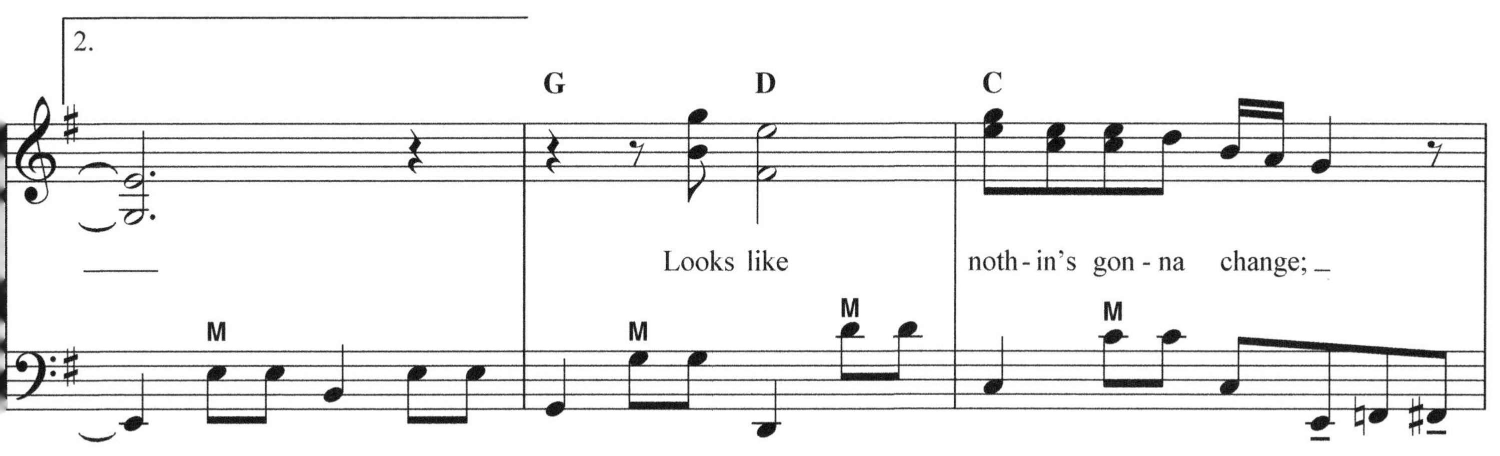
2.
G
D
C
Looks like noth - in's gon - na change;
M
M
M
M

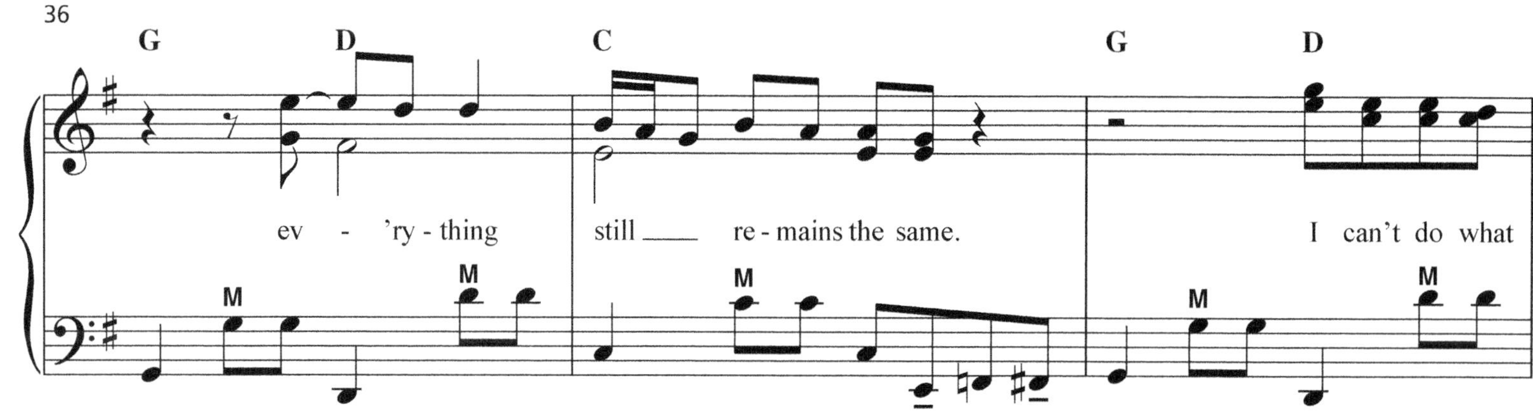
G
D
C
G
D
ev - 'ry - thing still re - mains the same. I can't do what
M
M
M
M
M

C
G
F
D
D.S. al Coda
ten peo - ple tell me to do, so I guess I'll re - main the same.
M
M
M

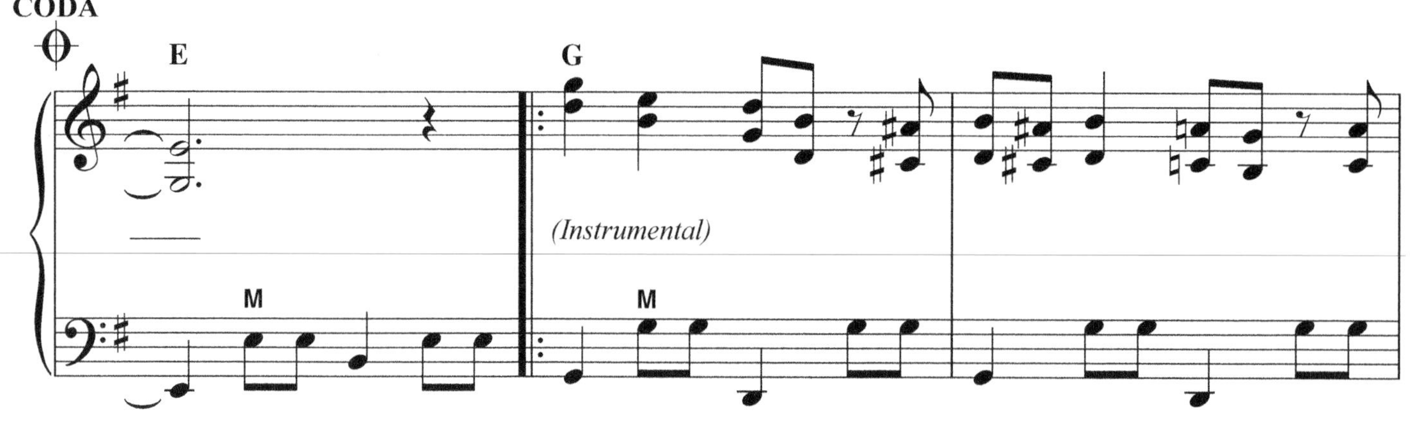
CODA
E
G
(Instrumental)
M
M

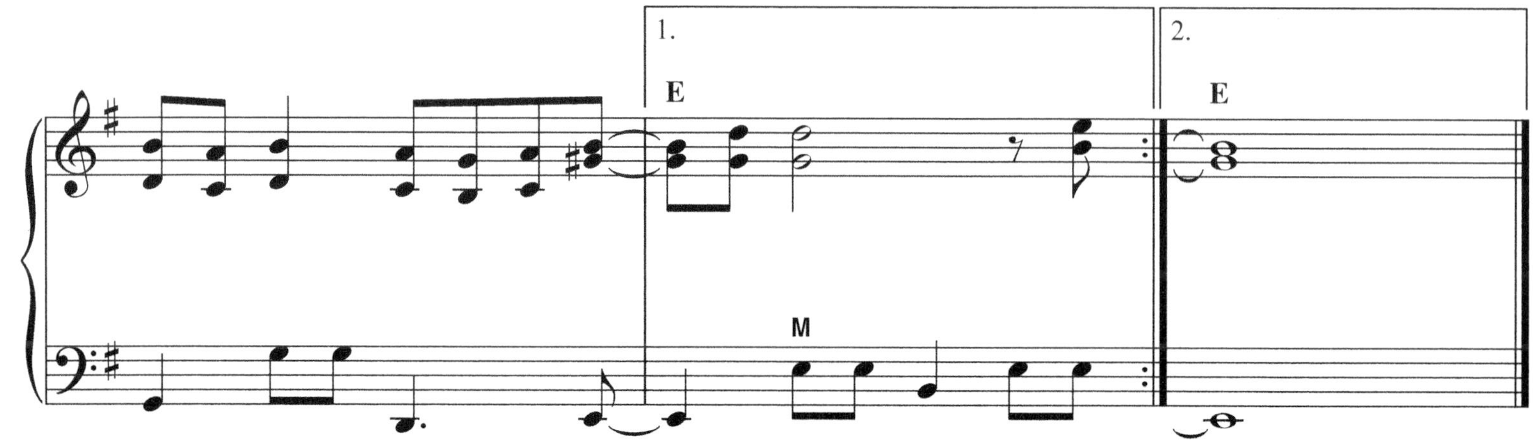
1.
2.
E
E
M

SPANISH HARLEM

Words and Music by JERRY LEIBER
and PHIL SPECTOR

3
up in Span - ish Har - lem.

F
It is a spec - ial one it's nev - er seen the sun. It on - ly
With eyes as black as coal that look down in my soul, and start a
M

C
comes out when the moon is on the run and all the stars are gleam - ing.
fire there and then I lose con - trol, I have to beg your par - don.
M

G
It's grow - ing in the street right up
I'm going to pick that rose and watch
M

1.
C
thru the con - crete but soft and sweet _ and dream - ing.
M
2.
C
her as she grows ______ in my gar - den.
M

SONG SUNG BLUE

Words and Music by
NEIL DIAMOND

Swing feel

F Dm Gm C7 F/A A♭dim Gm C7

Master

mf

M m m 7 m 7

Master

F C

Song sung blue, ev - 'ry - bod - y knows one.
Song sung blue, weep - in' like a wil - low.

M M

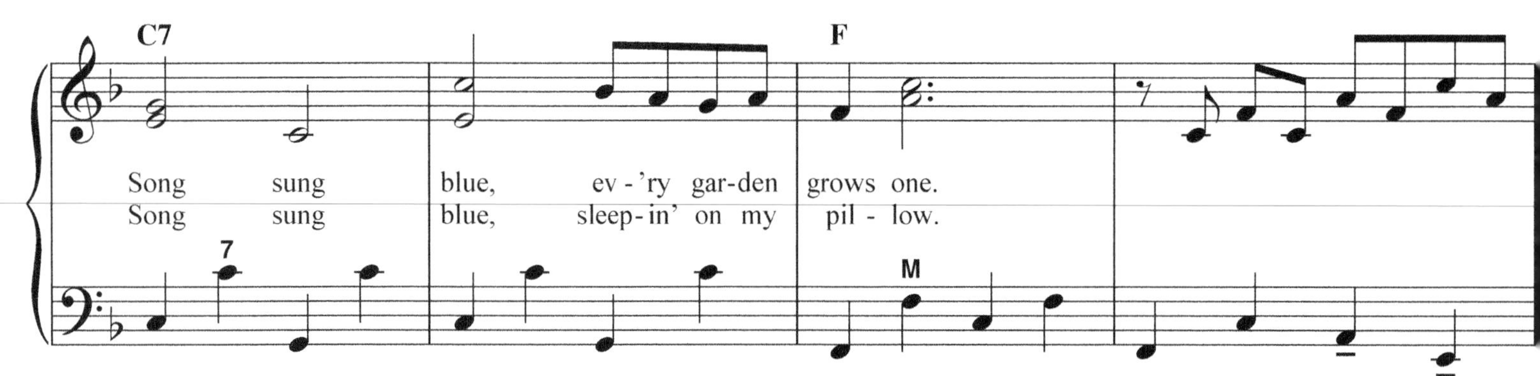

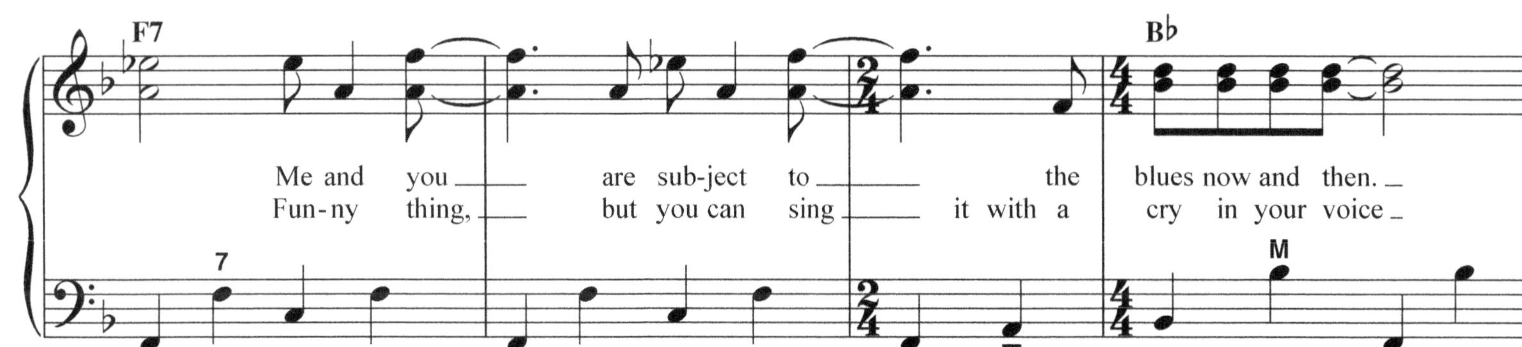

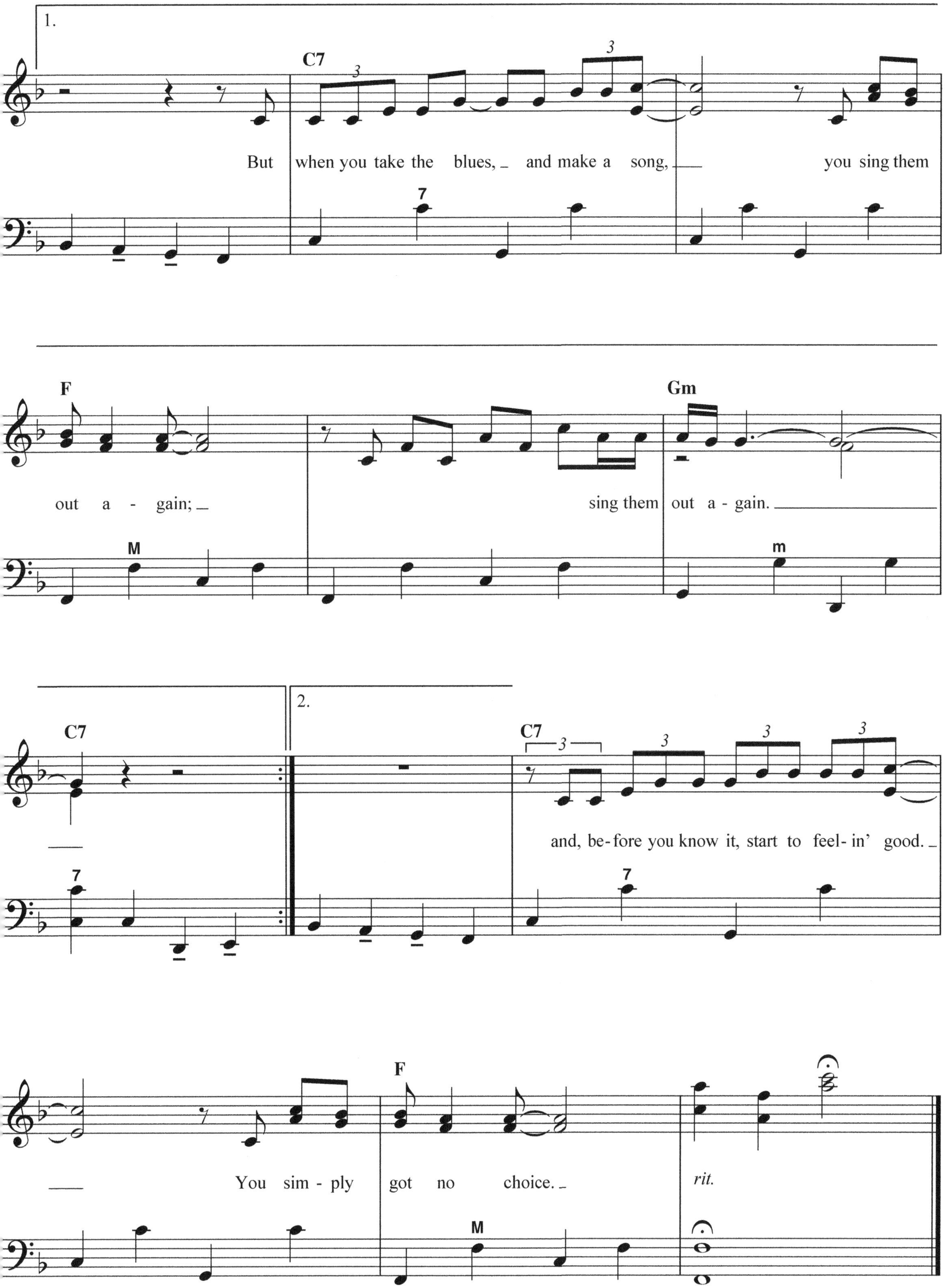

1.

C7

But when you take the blues, and make a song, you sing them

7

F

Gm

out a - gain; sing them out a - gain.

M

m

SPEAK SOFTLY, LOVE

(Love Theme)

from the Paramount Picture THE GODFATHER

Words by LARRY KUSIK
Music by NINO ROTA

E♭
D♭
G
sun, deep vel - vet nights when we are one. Speak soft - ly,
M
M
M

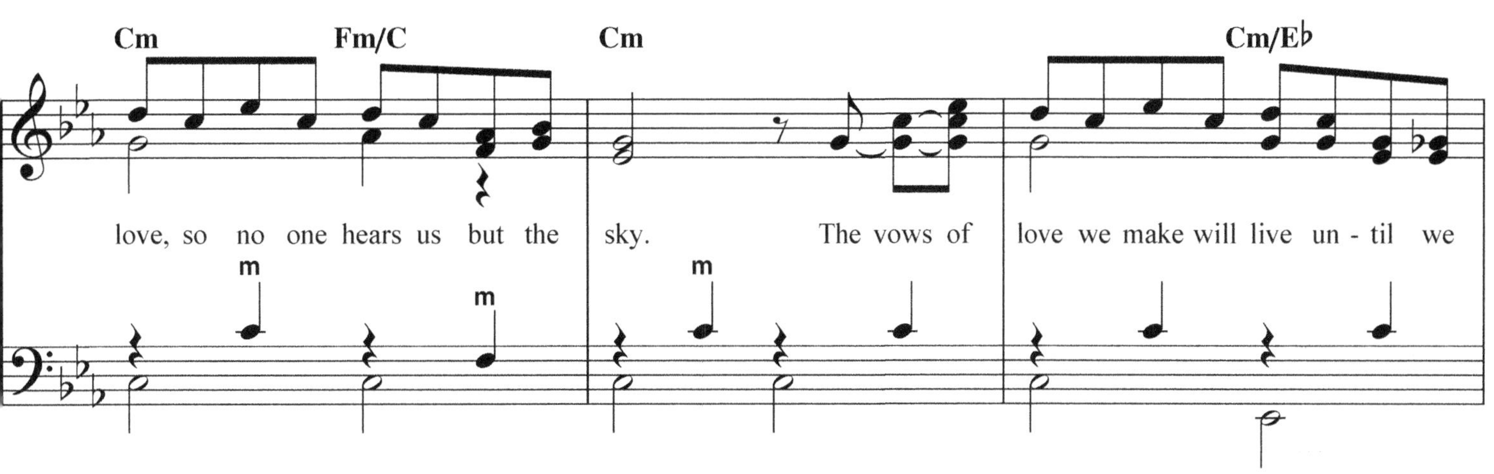
Cm
Fm/C
Cm
Cm/E♭
love, so no one hears us but the sky. The vows of love we make will live un - til we
m
m
m

Fm
Fdim
Cm
die. My life is yours and all be - cause you came in -
m
dim
m

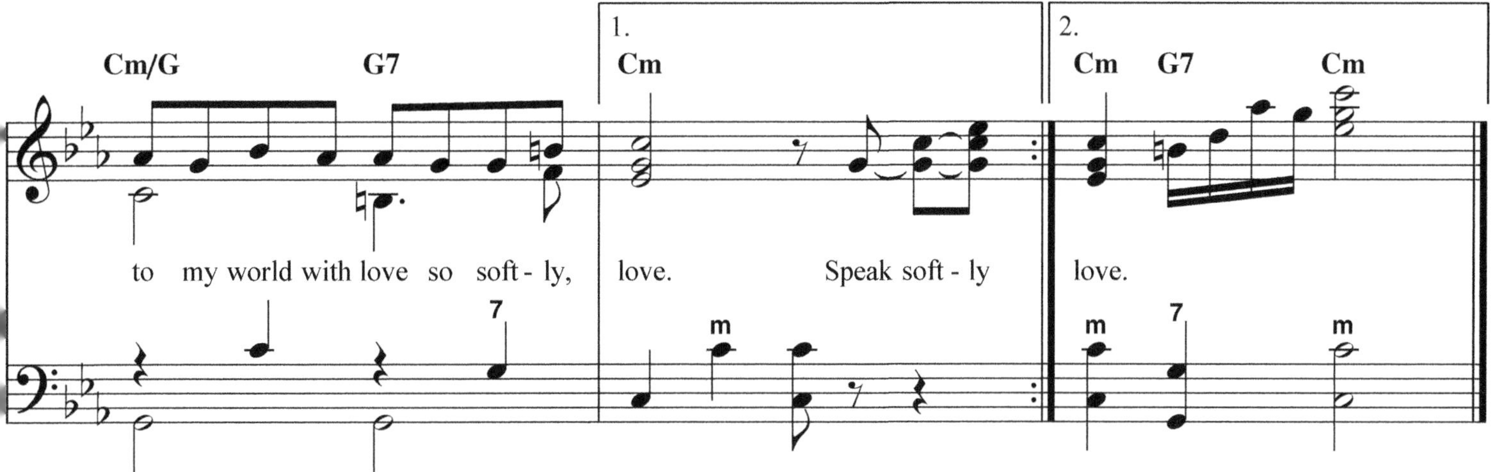
1.
2.
Cm/G
G7
Cm
Cm
G7
Cm
to my world with love so soft - ly, love. Speak soft - ly love.
7
m
m
7
m

SUNNY

Words and Music by
BOBBY HEBB

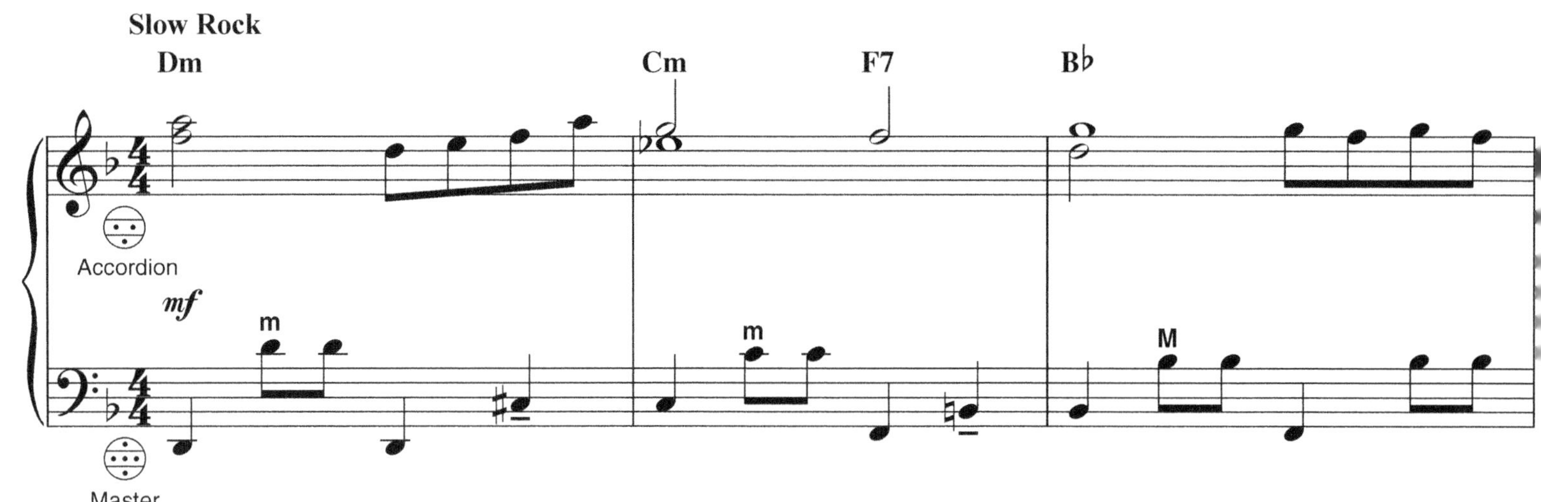

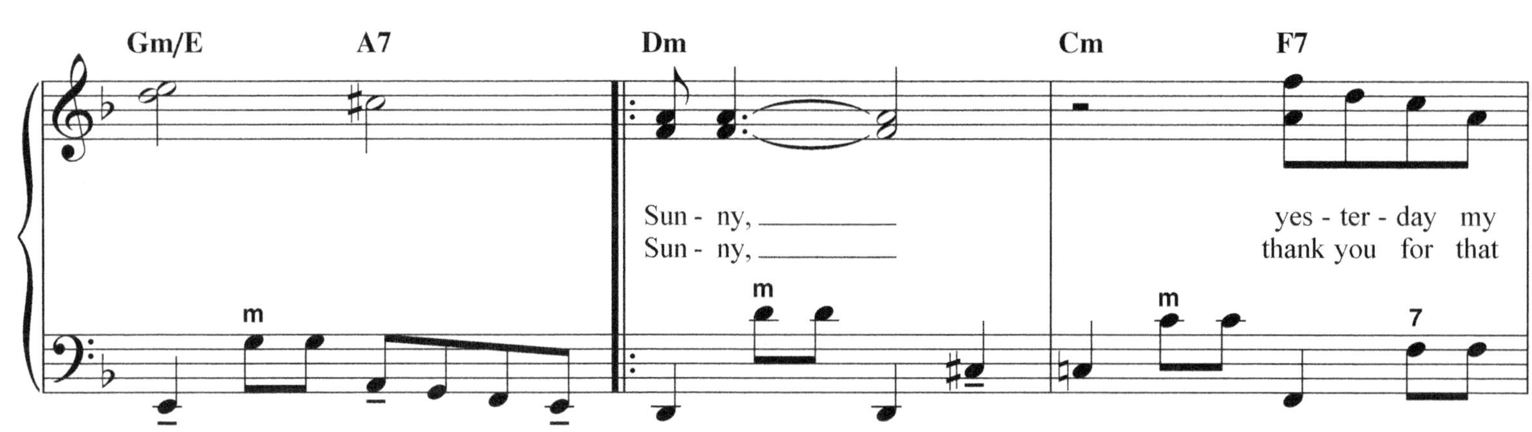

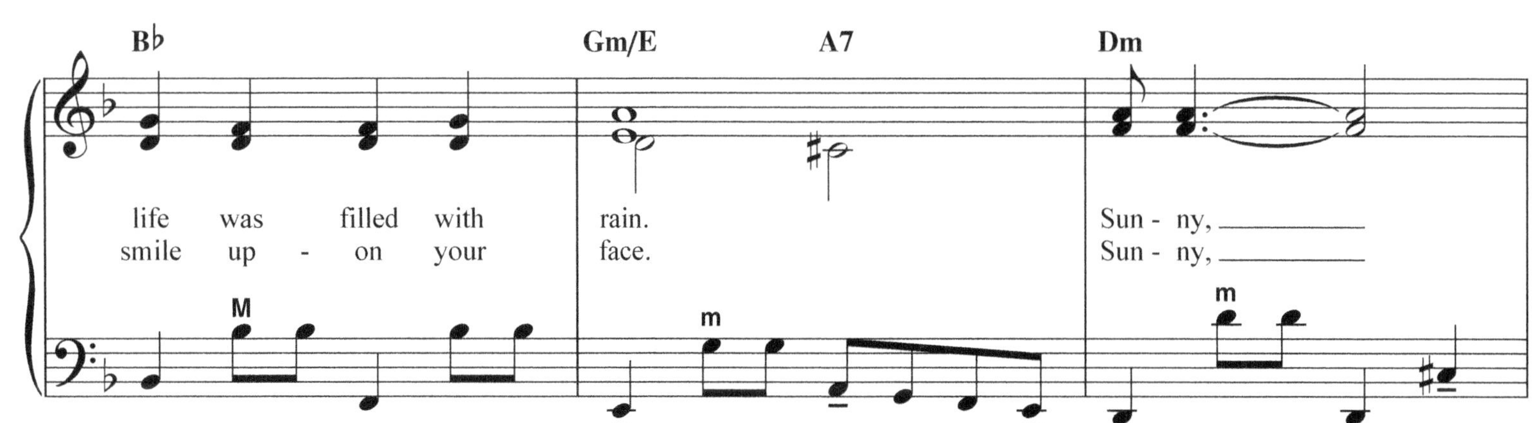

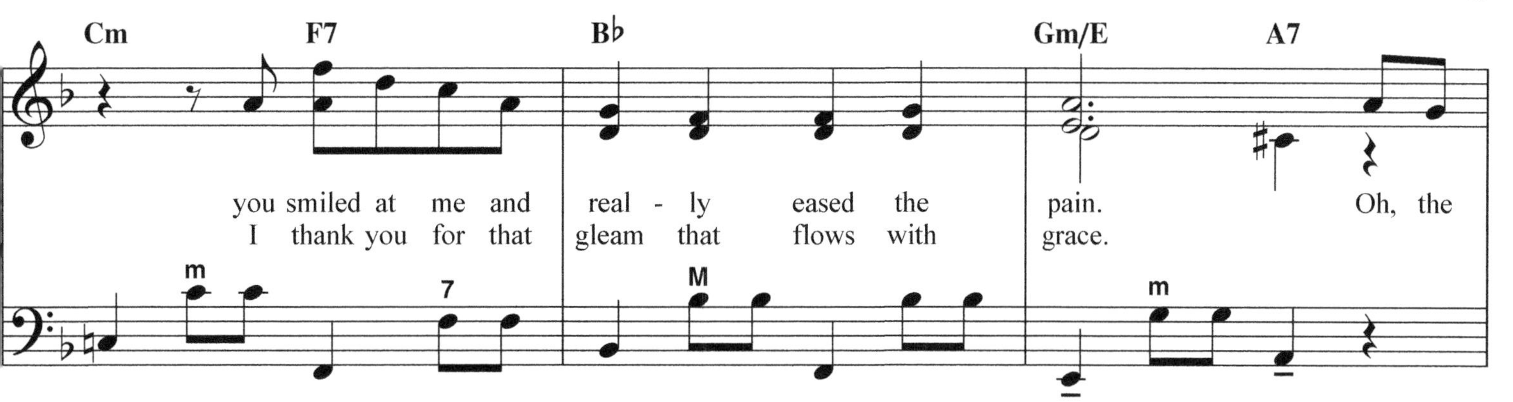
Cm
F7
B♭
Gm/E
A7
you smiled at me and
I thank you for that
real - ly eased the
gleam that flows with
pain. Oh, the
grace.
m
7
M
m

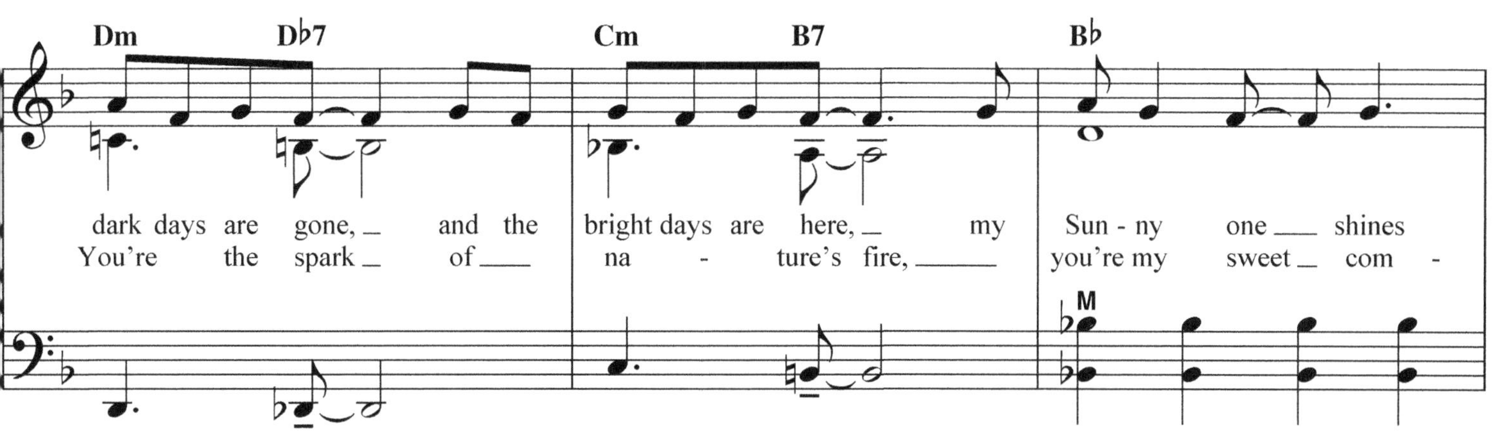
Dm
D♭7
Cm
B7
B♭
dark days are gone, and the
You're the spark of
bright days are here, my
na - ture's fire,
Sun - ny one shines
you're my sweet com -
M

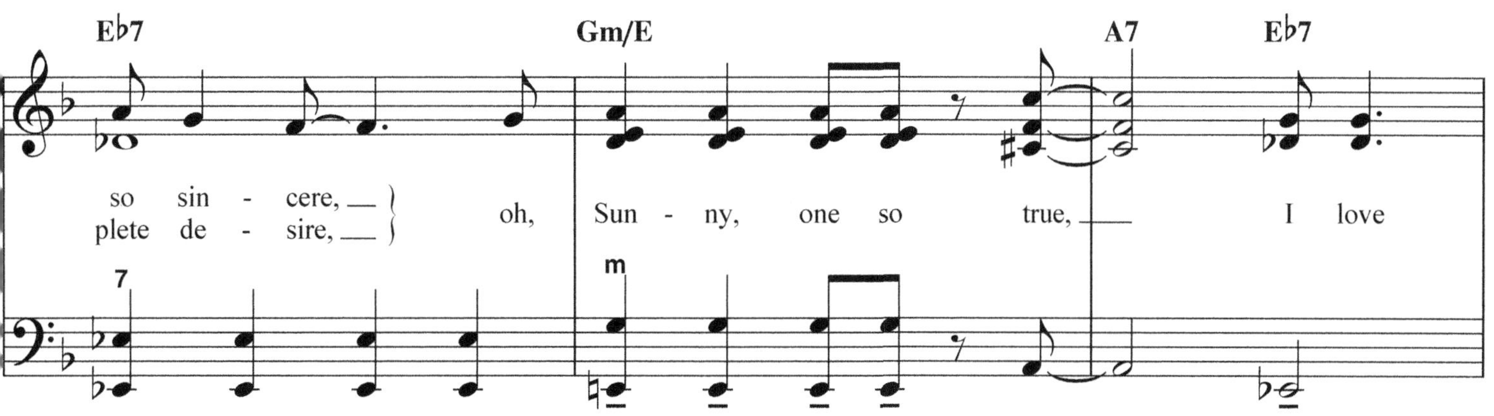
E♭7
Gm/E
A7
E♭7
so sin - cere,
plete de - sire,
oh,
Sun - ny, one so true,
I love
7
m

1.
Dm
B♭7
A7
you.
m
2.
Dm
B♭7
A7
Dm
you.
m
m

TAKE ME HOME, COUNTRY ROADS

Words and Music by JOHN DENVER,
BILL DANOFF and TAFFY NIVERT

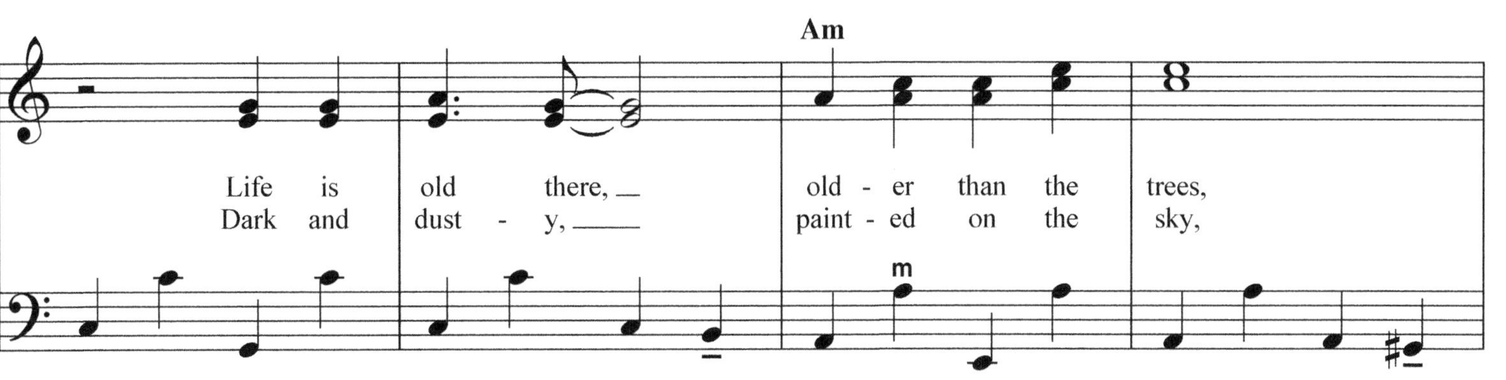
Am
Life is old there, older than the trees,
Dark and dust - y, paint - ed on the sky,
m

G
F♯
F
young - er than the moun - tains grow - in' like a breeze.
mist - y taste of moon - shine, tear - drop in my eye.
M
M

C
C
G
Coun - try roads, take me home
M
M
M

G♯dim
Am
F
to the place I be - long:
m
M

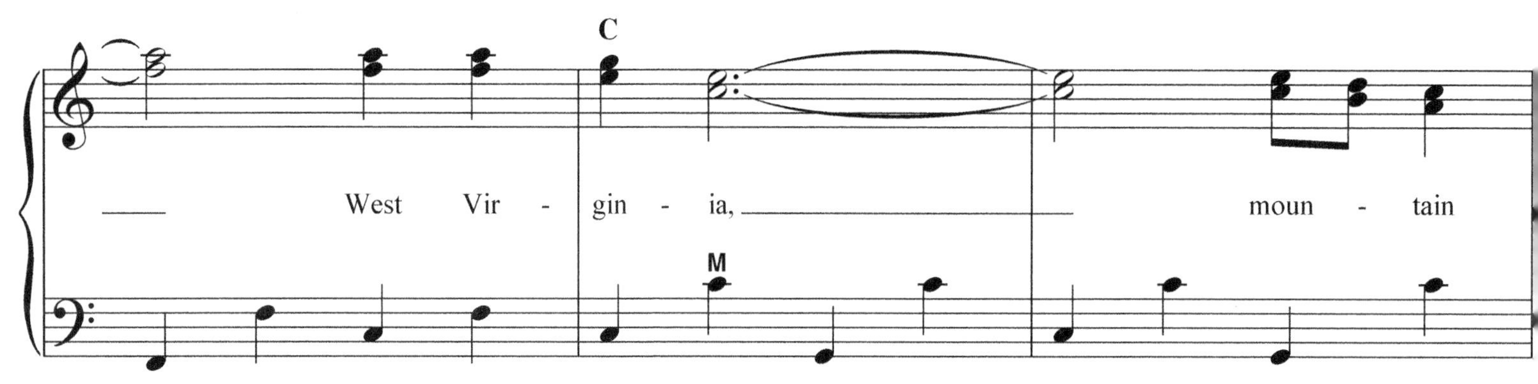
C
West Vir - gin - ia,
moun - tain
M

G
F
mom - ma.
Take me
home,
M
M
M

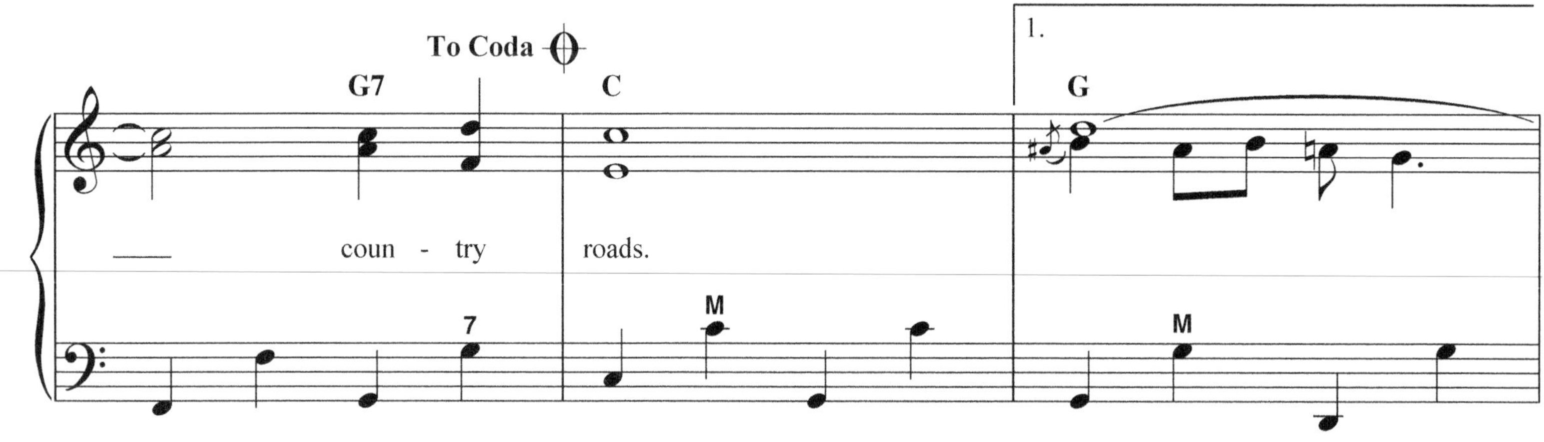
To Coda
G7
C
1.
G
coun - try
roads.
7
M
M

G7
2.
Am
All my
I hear her
7
m

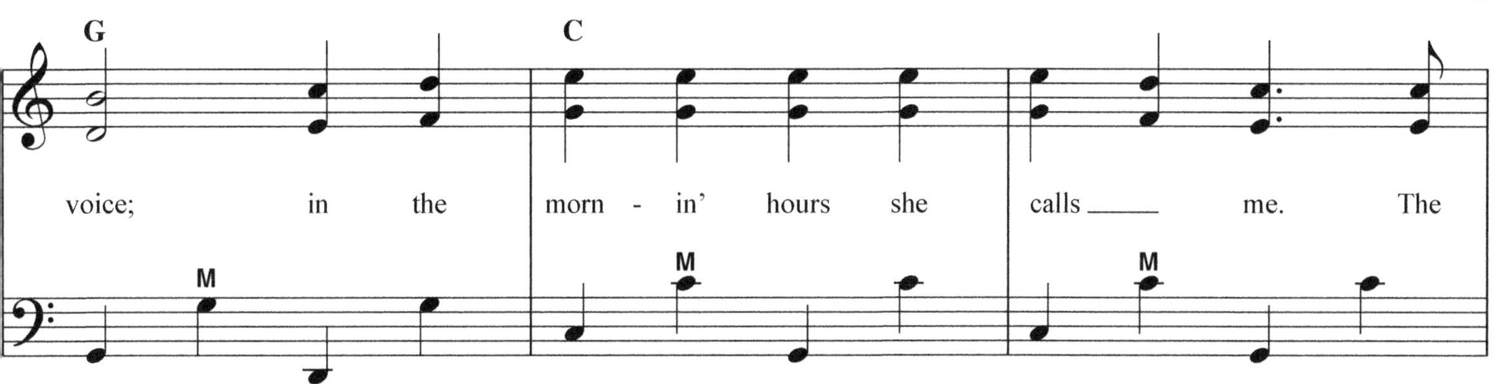
G
C
voice; in the morn - in' hours she calls ___ me. The
M
M
M

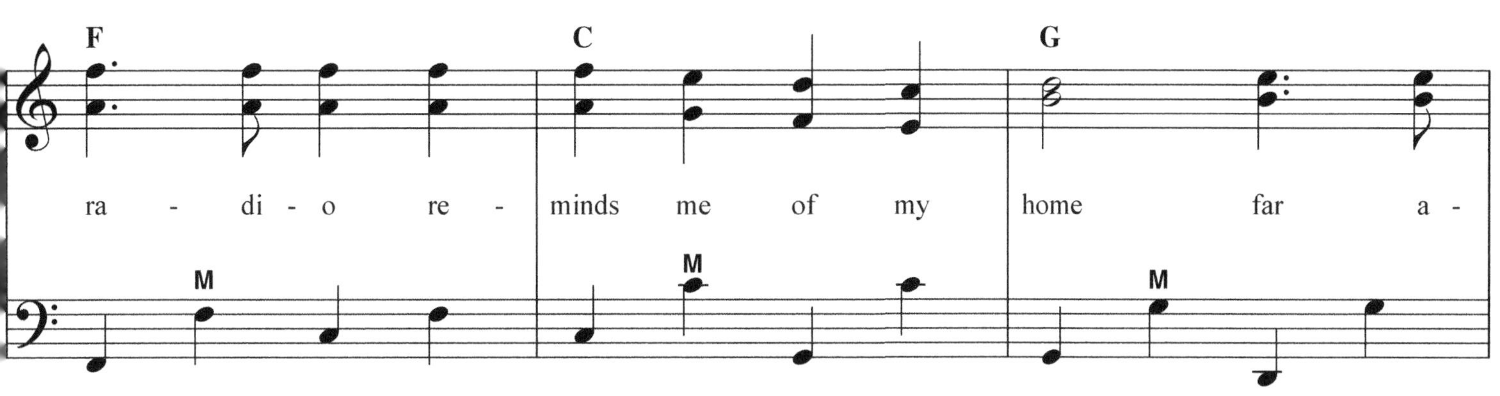
F
C
G
ra - di - o re - minds me of my home far a -
M
M
M

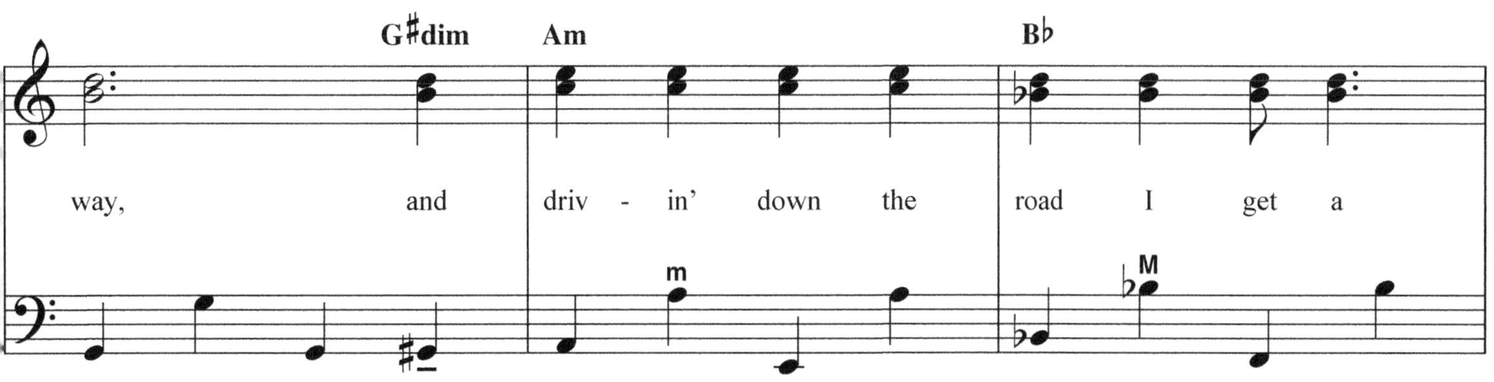
G♯dim
Am
B♭
way, and driv - in' down the road I get a
m
M

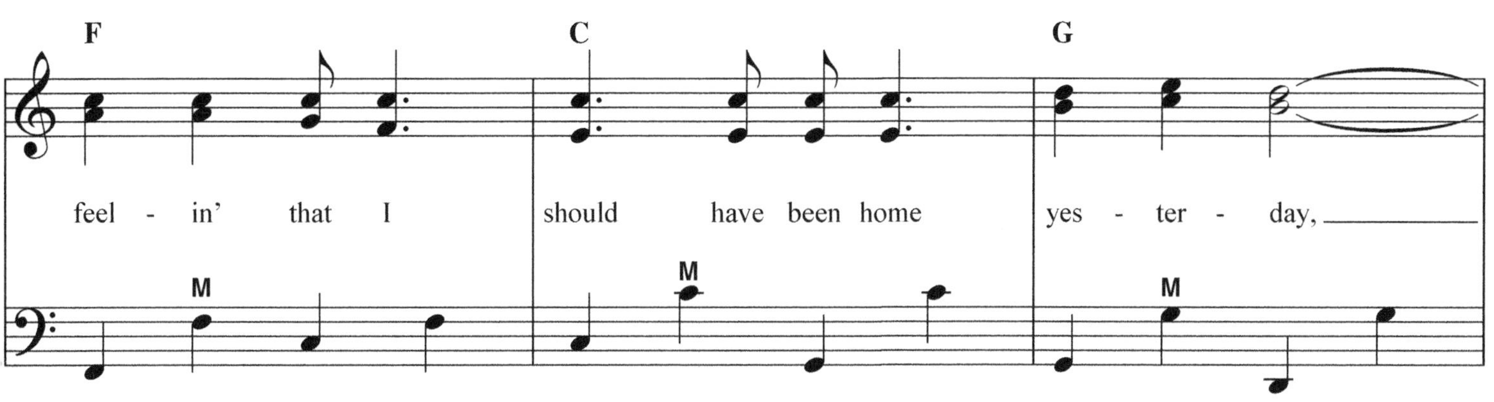
F
C
G
feel - in' that I should have been home yes - ter - day, ___
M
M
M

G7
D.S. al Coda
yes - ter - day.
Coun - try
7

CODA
C
G7
roads.
Take me
home,
M
7

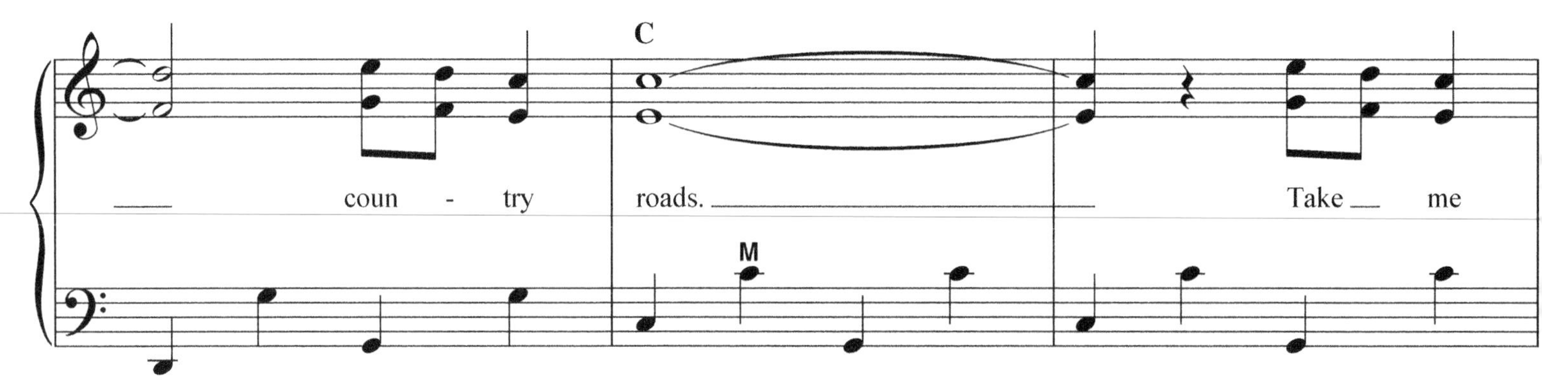
C
coun - try
roads.
Take me
M

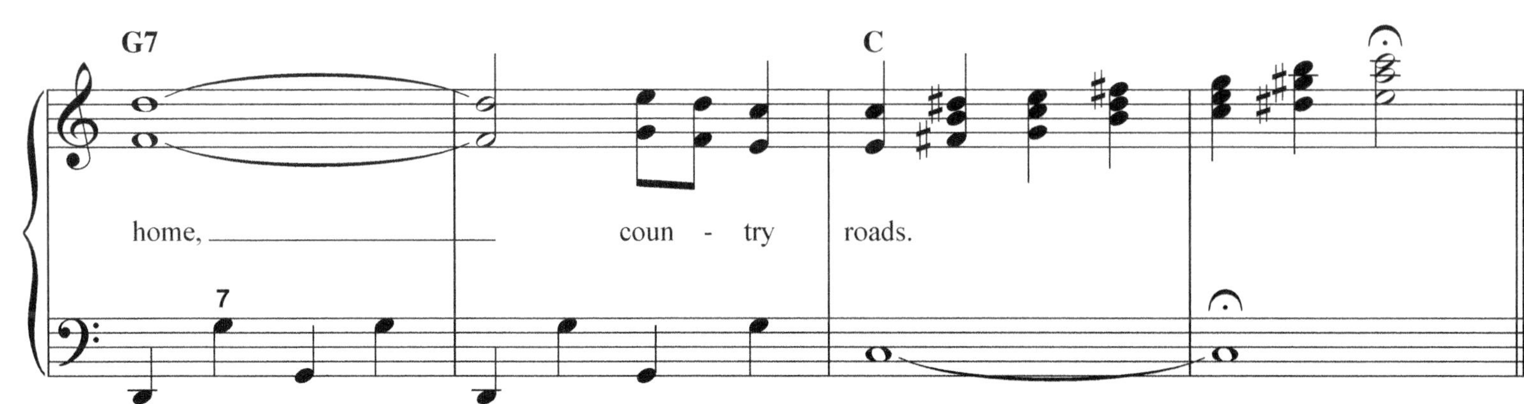
G7
C
home,
coun - try
roads.
7

UNCHAINED MELODY

Lyric by HY ZARET
Music by ALEX NORTH

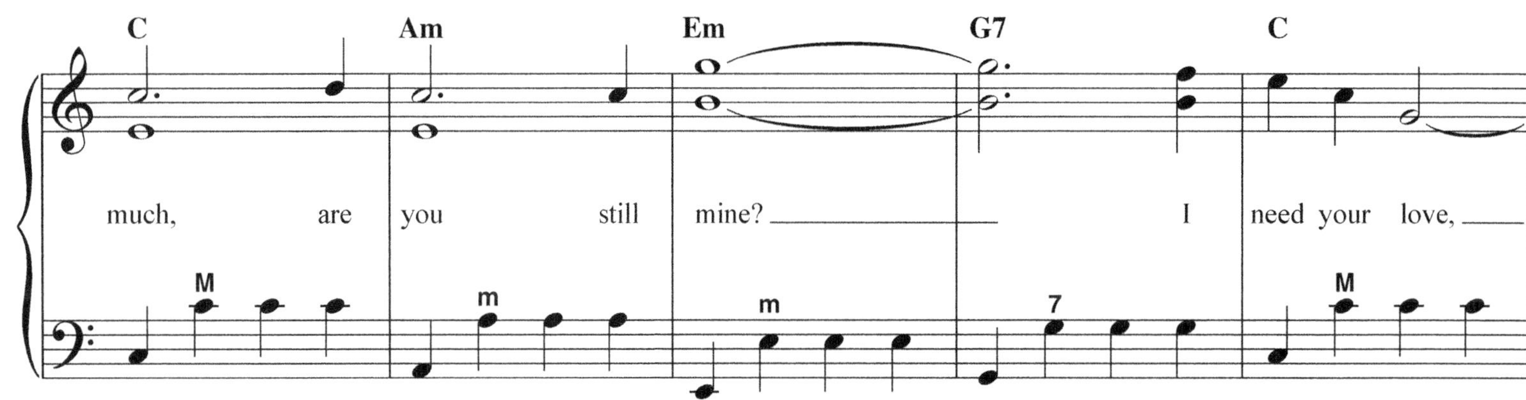
C
Am
Em
G7
C
much, are you still mine? I need your love,
M
m
m
7
M

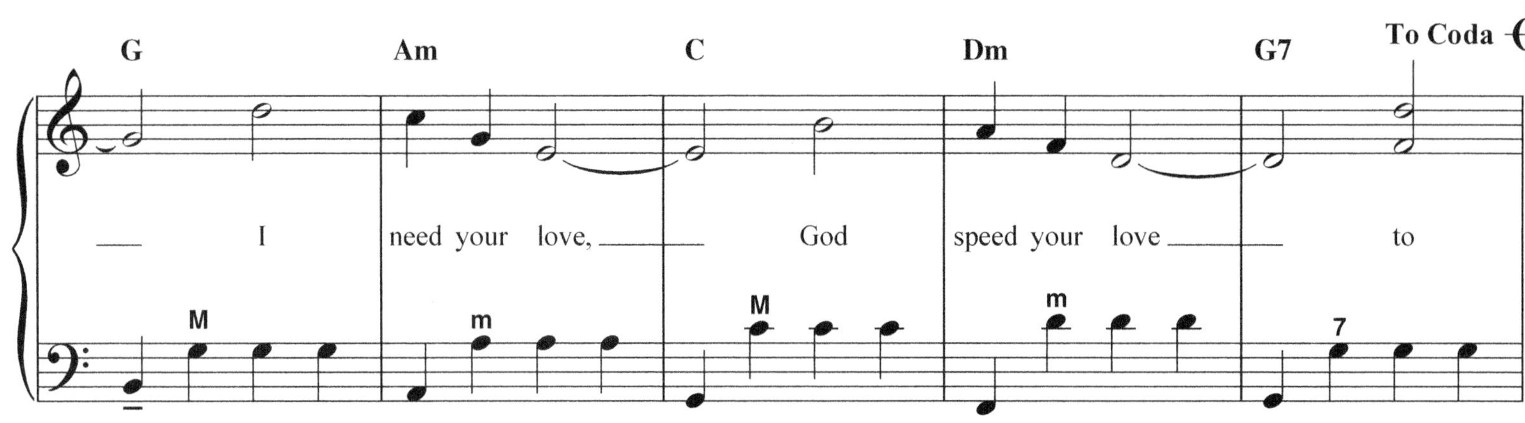
G
Am
C
Dm
G7
To Coda
I need your love, God speed your love to
M
m
M
m
7

C
F
G
me!
Lone - ly riv - ers flow to the
Lone - ly moun - tains gaze at the
M
M
M

F
E♭
F
G
sea, to the sea, to the o - pen arms of the
stars, at the stars, wait - ing for the dawn of the
M
M
M
M

C
F
G
sea.
day.
Lone - ly riv - ers sigh, "Wait for
All a - lone, I gaze at the
M

F
E♭
F
G
me, wait for me!" I'll be com - ing home wait for
stars, at the stars, dream - ing of my love far a -
M

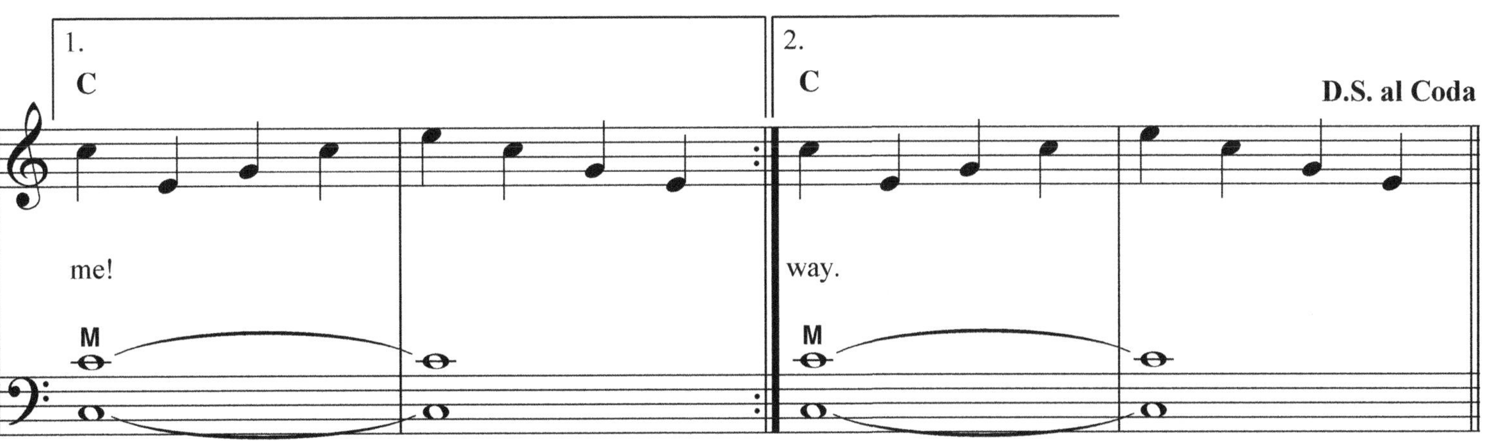
1.
2.
C
D.S. al Coda
me!
way.
M

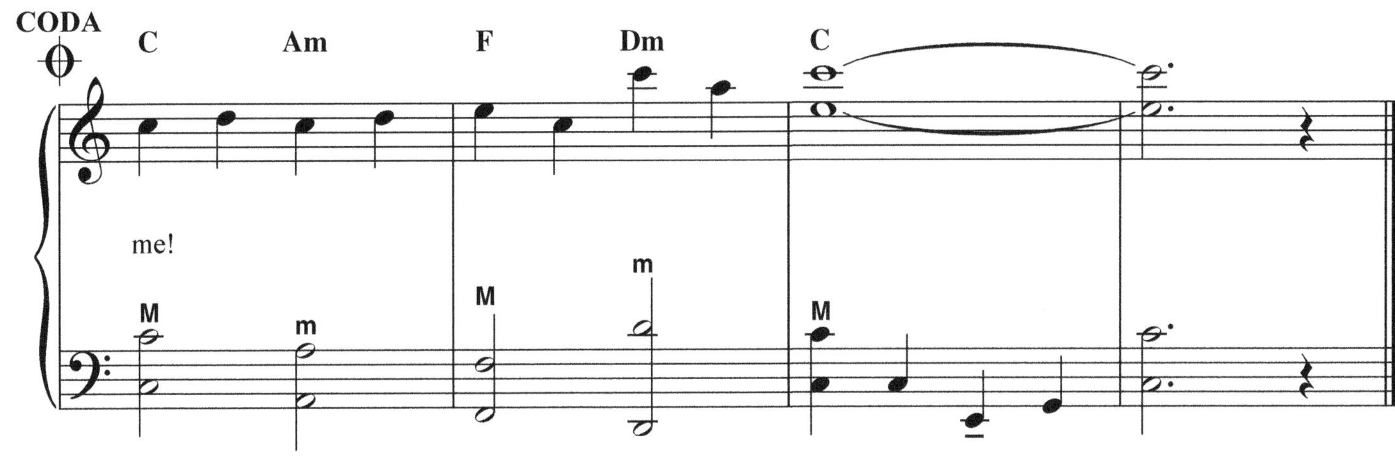
CODA
C
Am
F
Dm
me!
M
m

THAT'S AMORÉ
(That's Love)
from the Paramount Picture THE CADDY

Words by JACK BROOKS
Music by HARRY WARREN

Quick Waltz

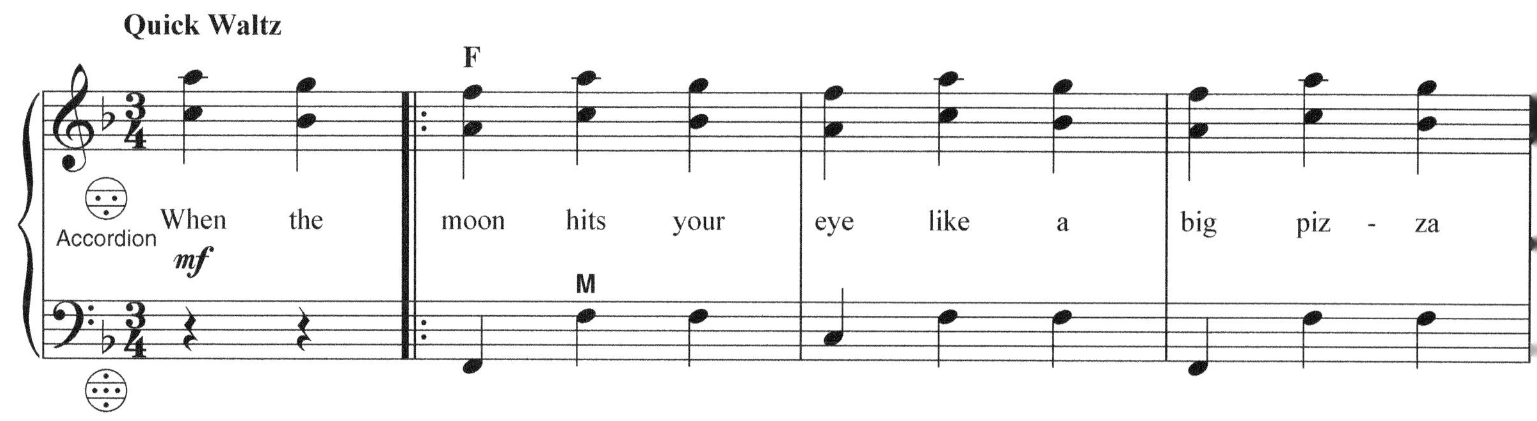

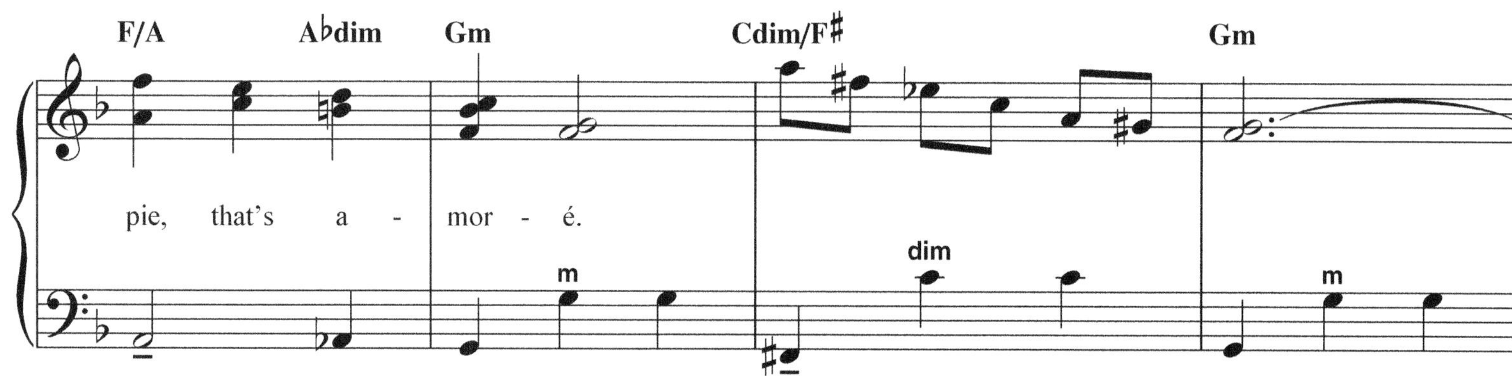

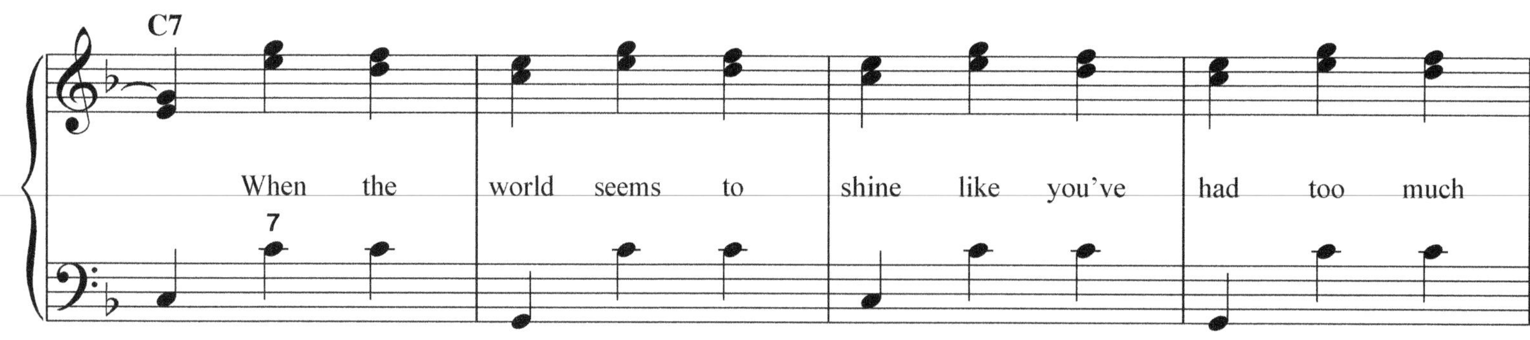

A♭dim
ring, ting - a - ling - a - ling, ting - a - ling - a - ling, and you'll sing, Vee - ta -
dim

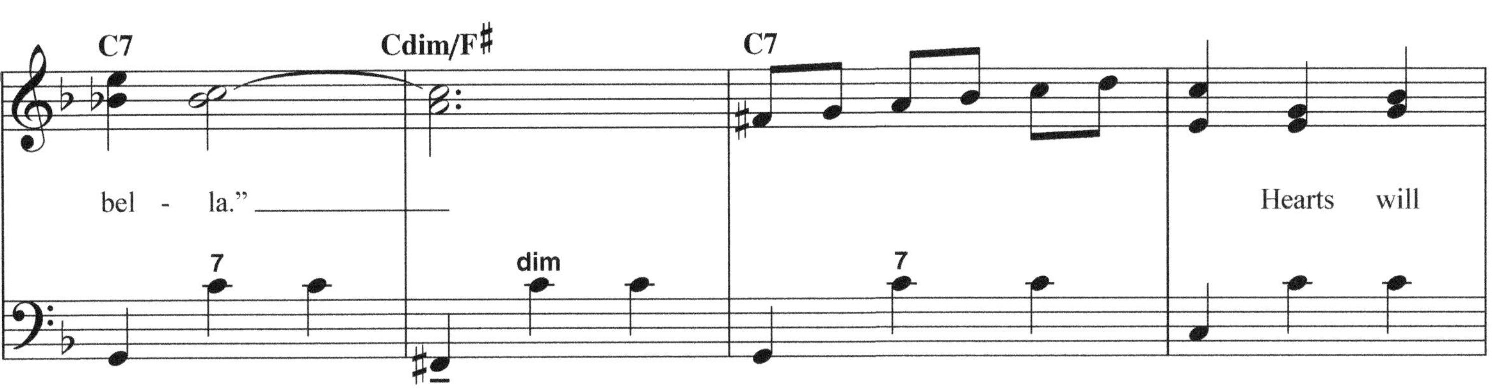
C7
Cdim/F♯
C7
bel - la."
Hearts will
7
dim
7

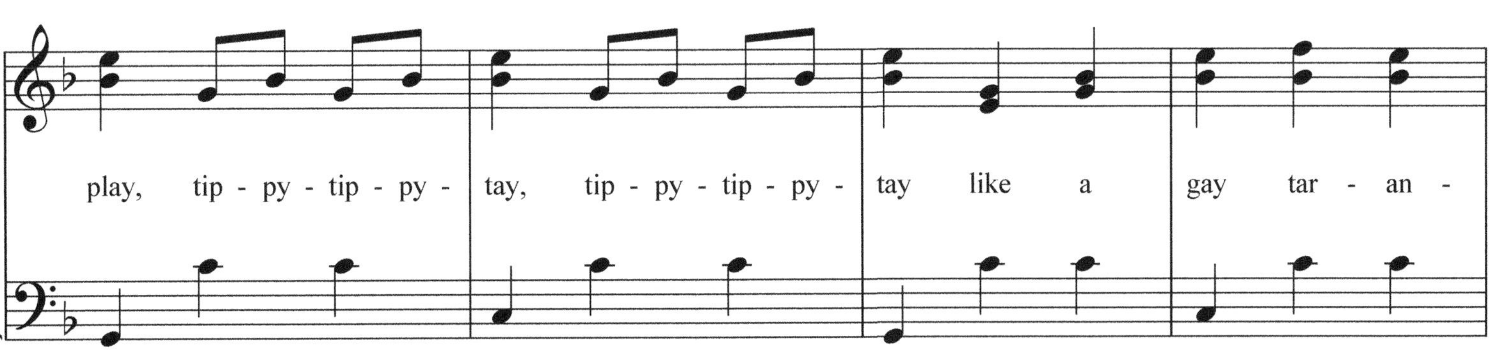
play, tip - py - tip - py - tay, tip - py - tip - py - tay like a gay tar - an -

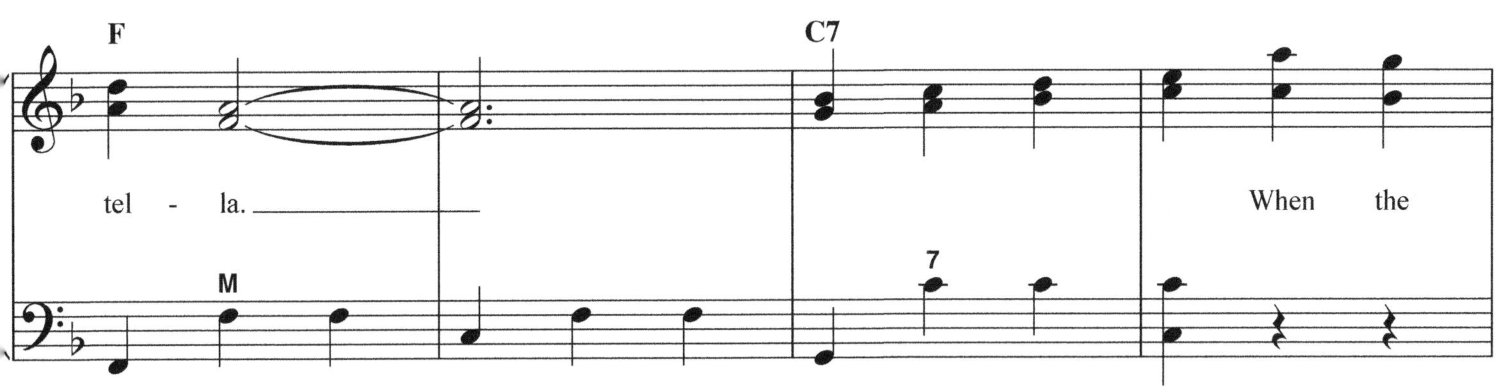
F
C7
tel - la.
When the
M
7

F
F/A
A♭dim
Gm
stars make you drool just like pas - ta fa - zool, that's a - mor - é.
M
m

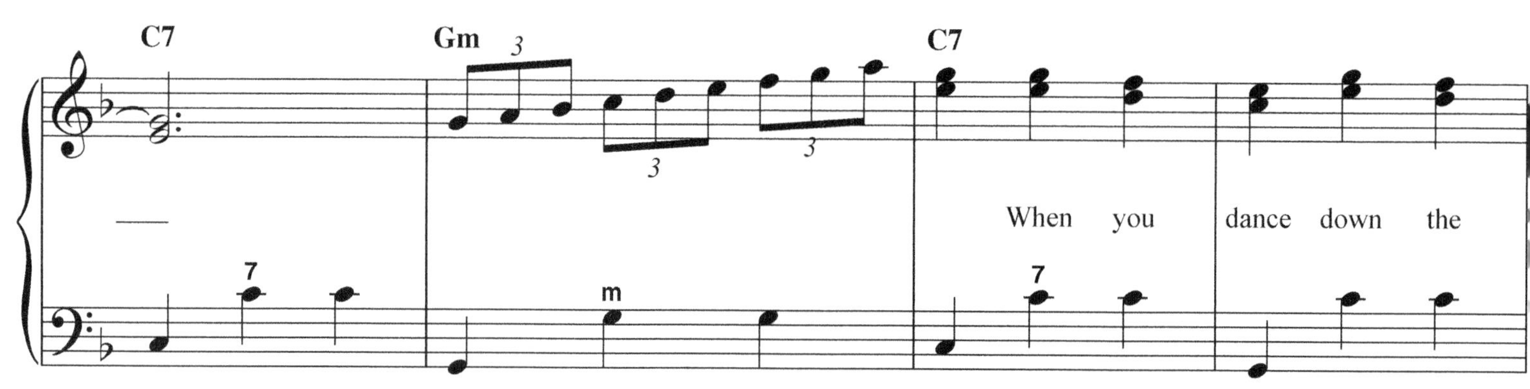
C7
Gm
3
3
3
C7
When you dance down the
7
m
7

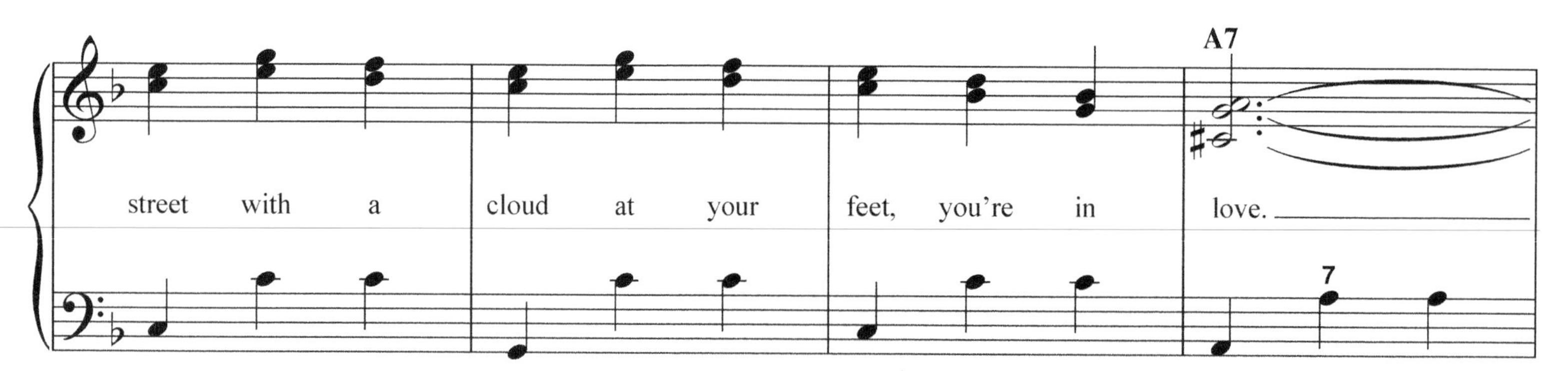
A7
street with a cloud at your feet, you're in love.
7

A7/E♭
D7
Gm
When you walk in a dream but you
7
m

Bbm
F
know you're not dream - ing, Sig - nor - é,
m
M

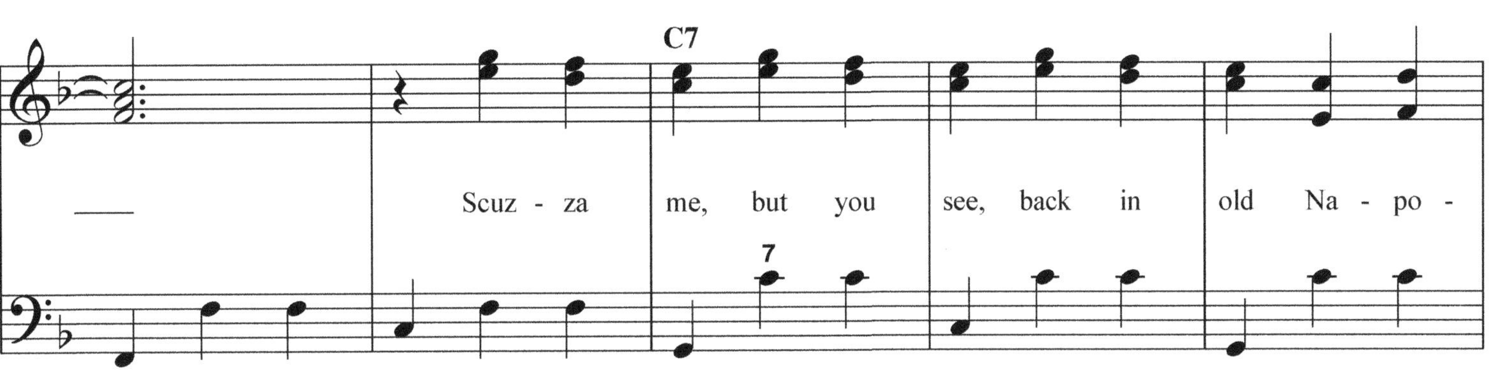
C7
Scuz - za me, but you see, back in old Na - po -
7

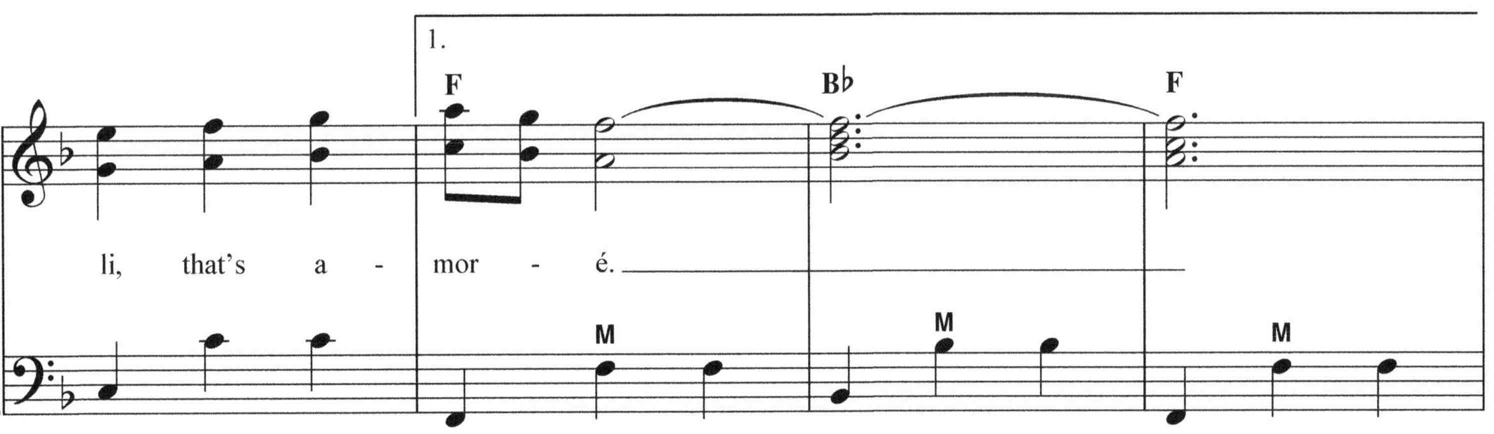
1.
F
Bb
F
li, that's a - mor - é.
M
M
M

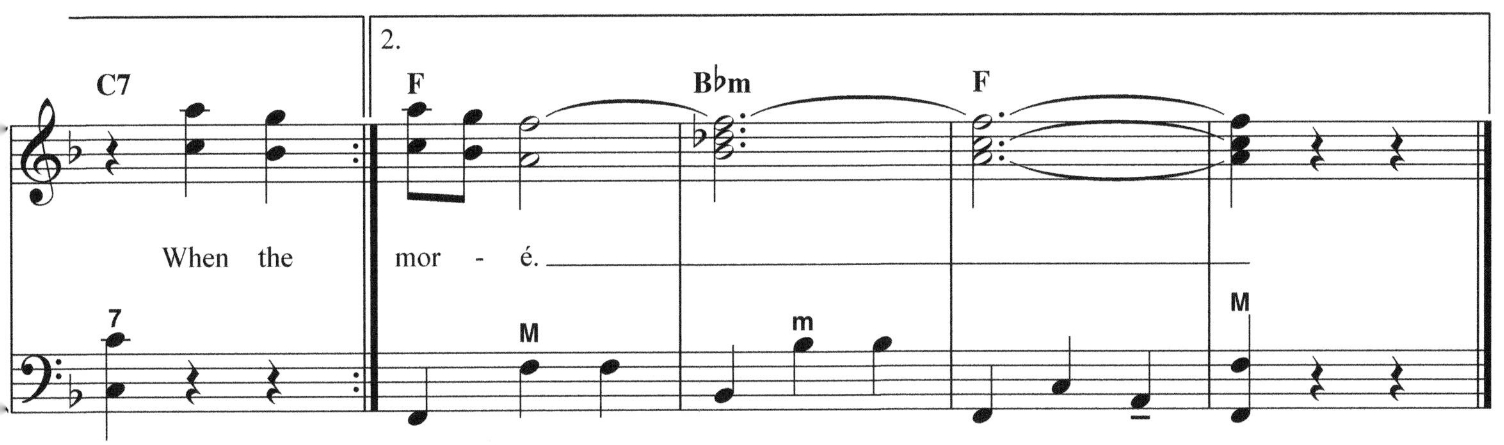
C7
2.
F
Bbm
F
When the mor - é.
7
M
m
M

WIVES AND LOVERS

(Hey, Little Girl)

from the Paramount Picture WIVES AND LOVERS

Words by HAL DAVID
Music by BURT BACHARACH

C7
Gm
fin - ger
you
need - n't
try
an - y -
more.
curl - ers,
you
may not
see
him
a -
gain.
7
m

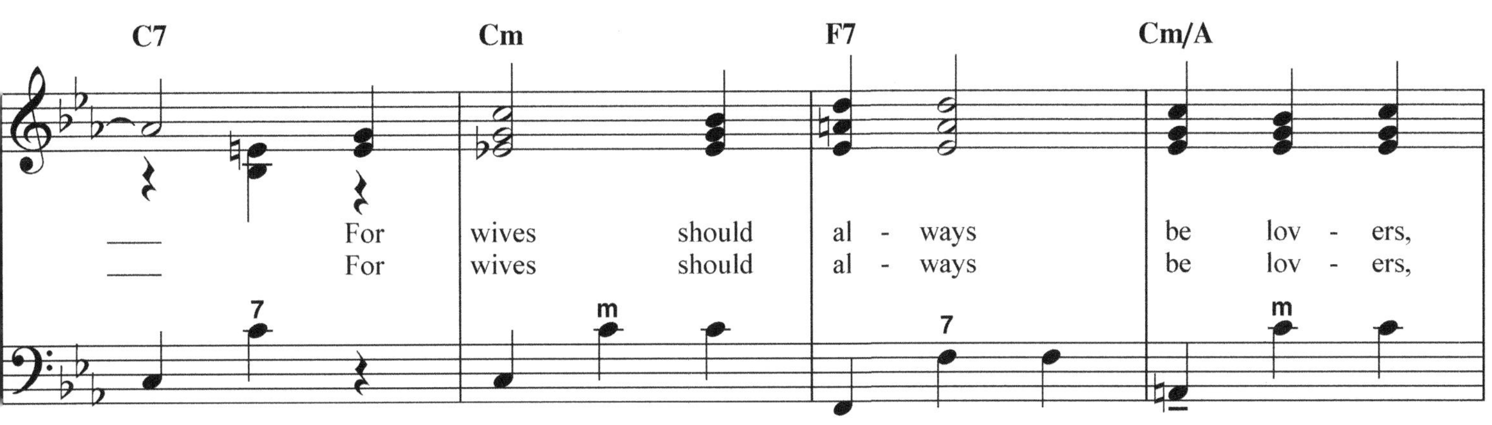
C7
Cm
F7
Cm/A
For
wives
should
al - ways
be
lov - ers,
For
wives
should
al - ways
be
lov - ers,
7
m
7
m

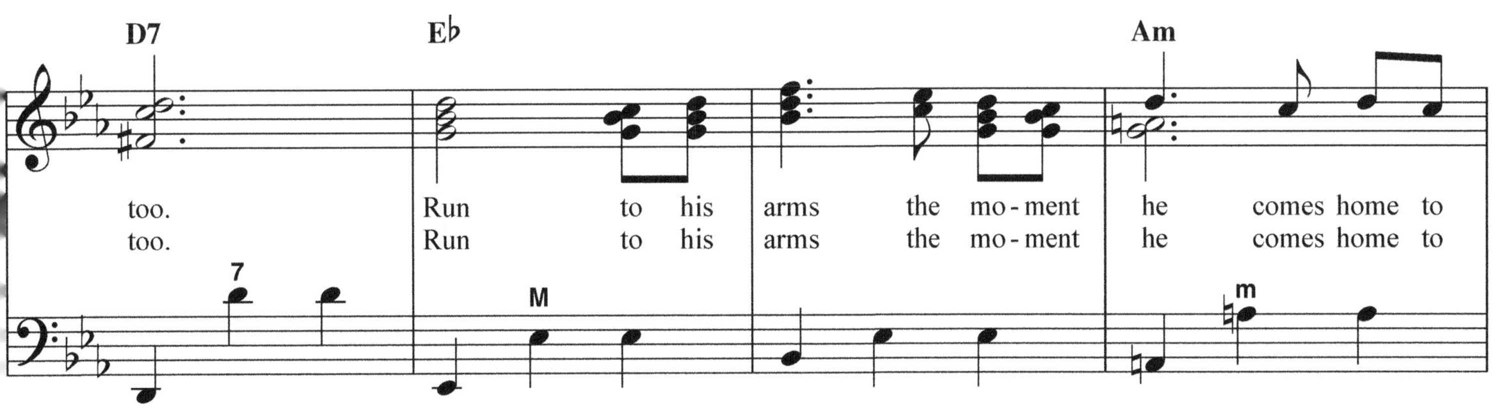
D7
E♭
Am
too.
Run
to his
arms
the mo - ment
he
comes home to
too.
Run
to his
arms
the mo - ment
he
comes home to
7
M
m

D7
D♭
Gm
C7
you.
I'm
warn - ing
you.
you.
He's
al - ways
here.
7
m
7
3
3

Fm
Bb7
Fm
Hey, lit - tle girl, bet - ter wear some - thing
m
7
m

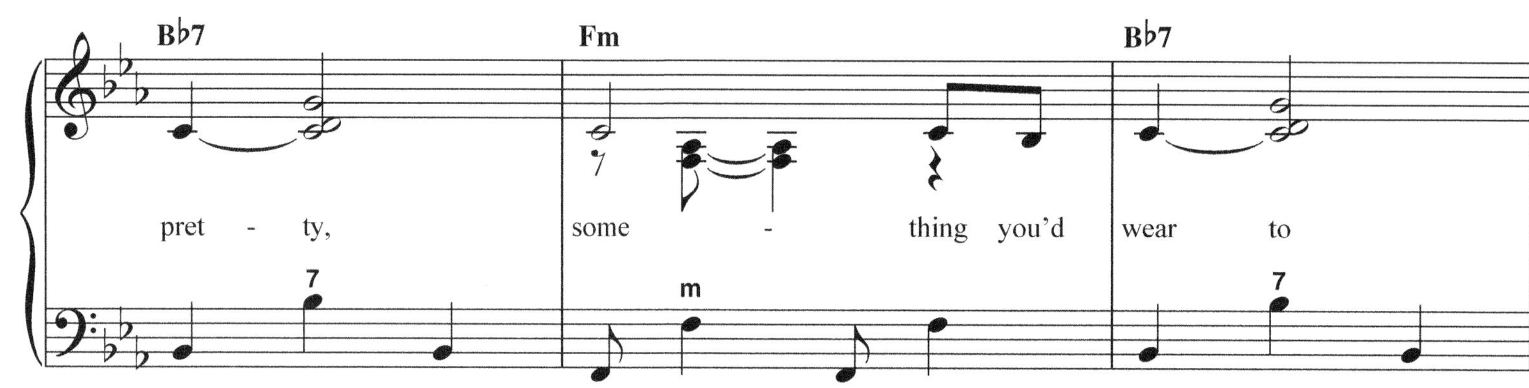
Bb7
Fm
Bb7
pret - ty, some - thing you'd wear to
7
m
7

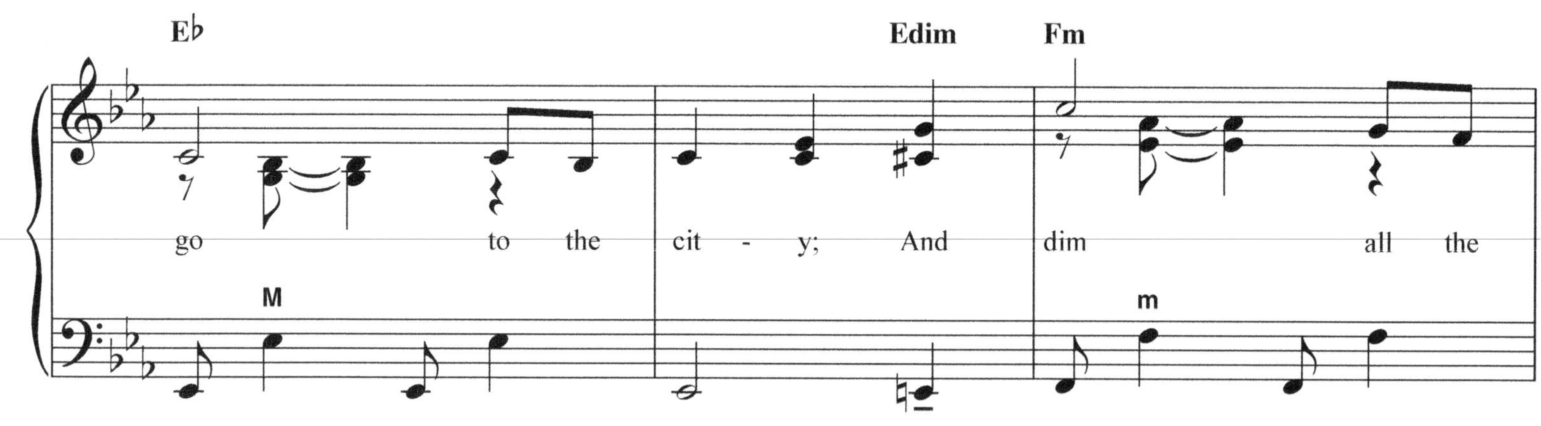
Eb
Edim
Fm
go to the cit - y; And dim all the
M
m

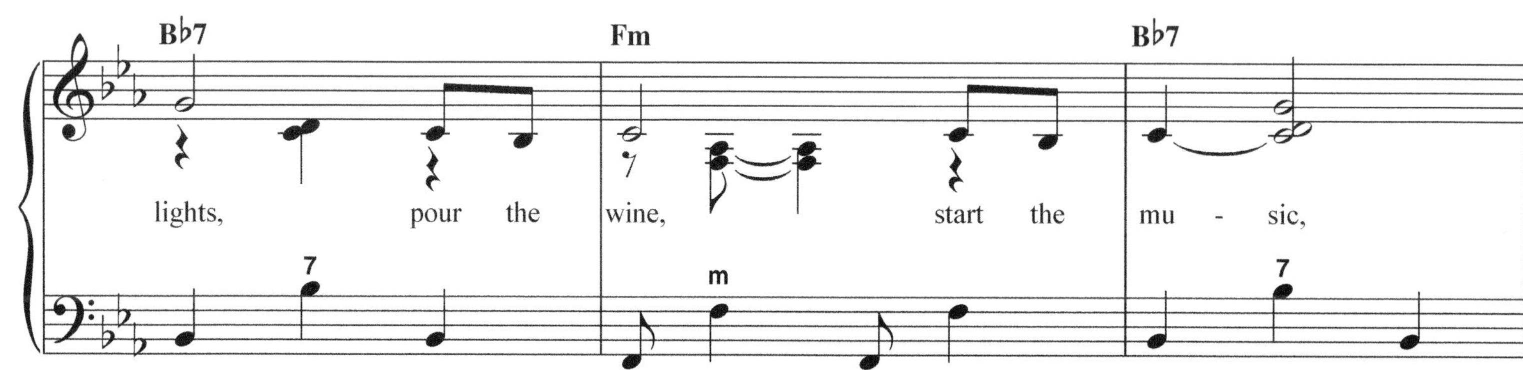
Bb7
Fm
Bb7
lights, pour the wine, start the mu - sic,
7
m
7

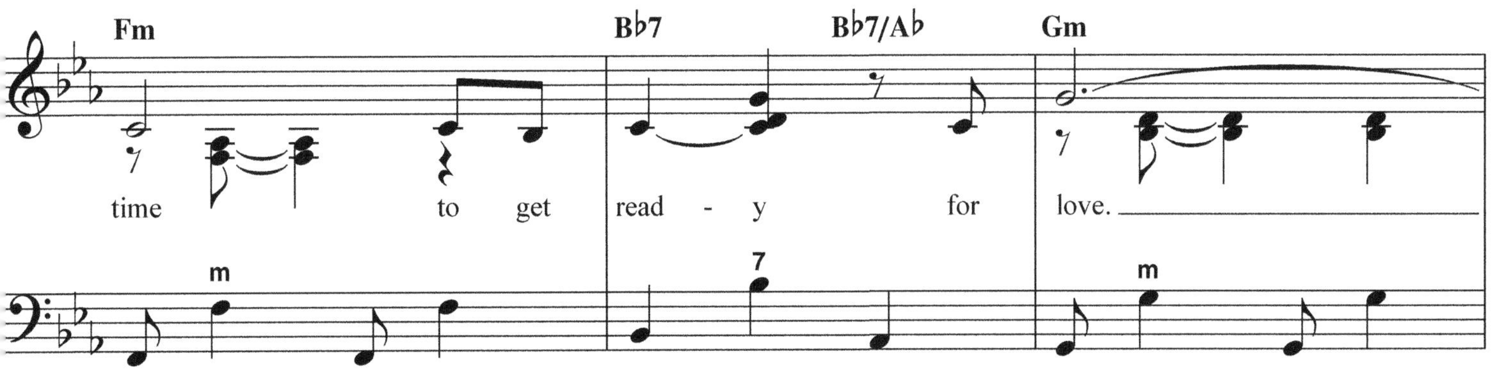
Fm
Bb7
Bb7/Ab
Gm
time to get read - y for love.
m
7
m

C7
Fm
Bb7
Oh, time to get read - y,
7
m
7

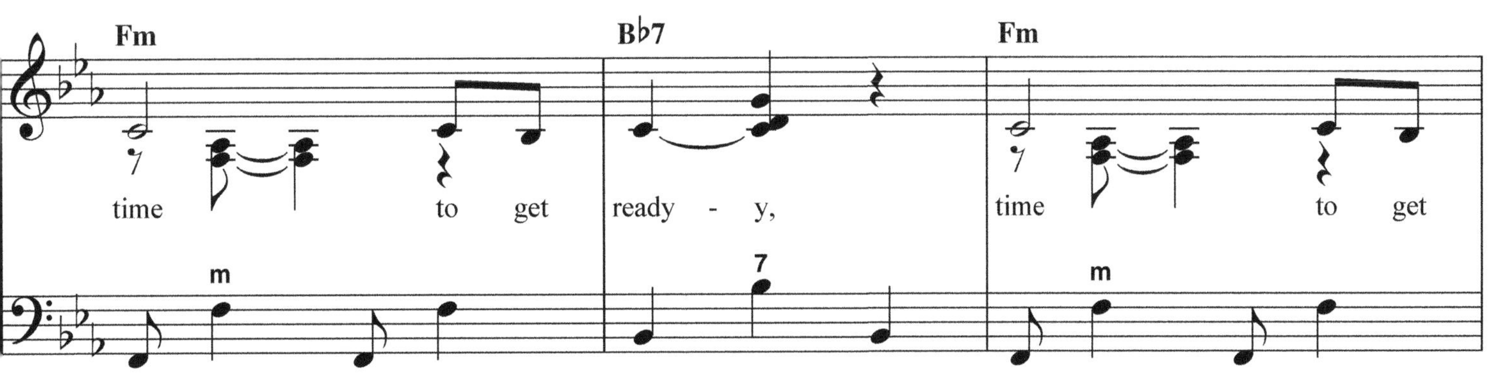
Fm
Bb7
Fm
time to get ready - y, time to get
m
7
m

Bb7
Eb
Db7
Eb
read - y for love.
7

WOODEN HEART

Words and Music by BEN WEISMAN,
FRED WISE, KAY TWOMEY
and BERTHOLD KAEMPFERT

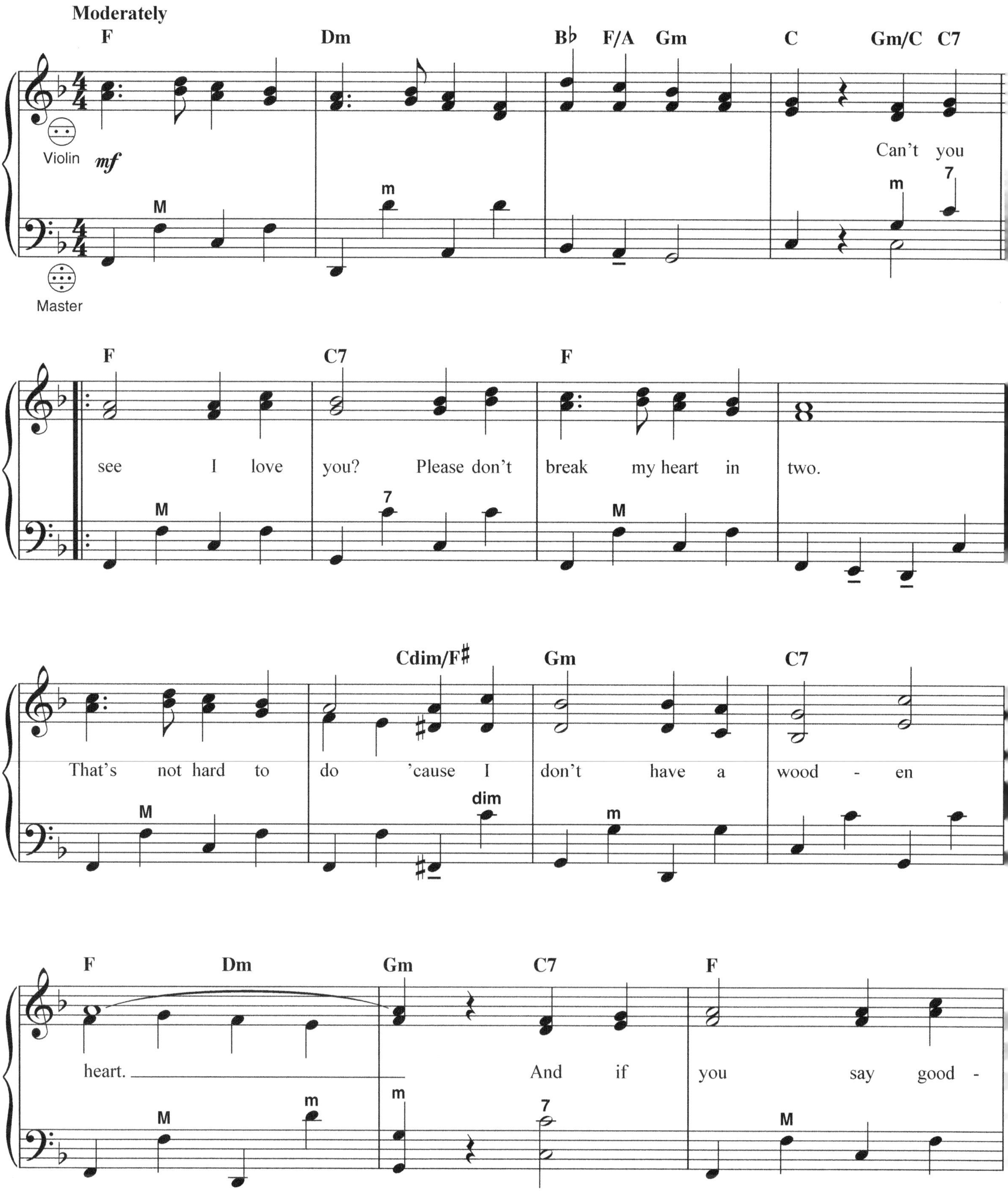

Moderately

F Dm B♭ F/A Gm C Gm/C C7

Violin *mf*

Can't you

M m m 7

Master

F C7 F

see I love you? Please don't break my heart in two.

M 7 M

Cdim/F♯ Gm C7

That's not hard to do 'cause I don't have a wood - en

M dim m

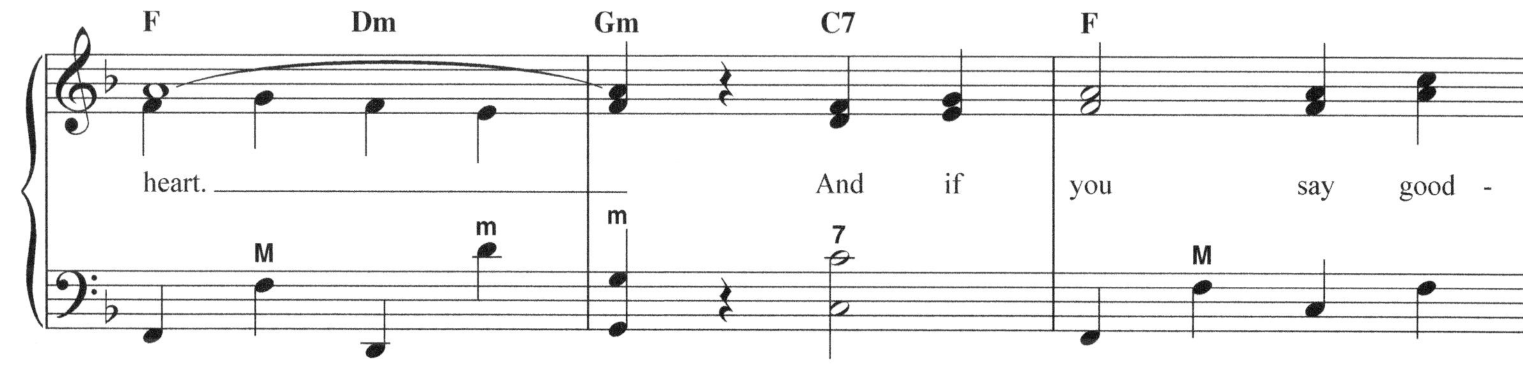

C7
F
bye, then I know that I would cry.
7
M

Cdim/F♯
Gm
May - be I would die 'cause I don't have a
dim
m

C7
F
Gm
Ddim/G♯
F/A
Dm
wood - en heart. There's no
7
M
m
dim
m

Gm
C7
F
F7
strings up - on this love of mine. It was
m
7
M

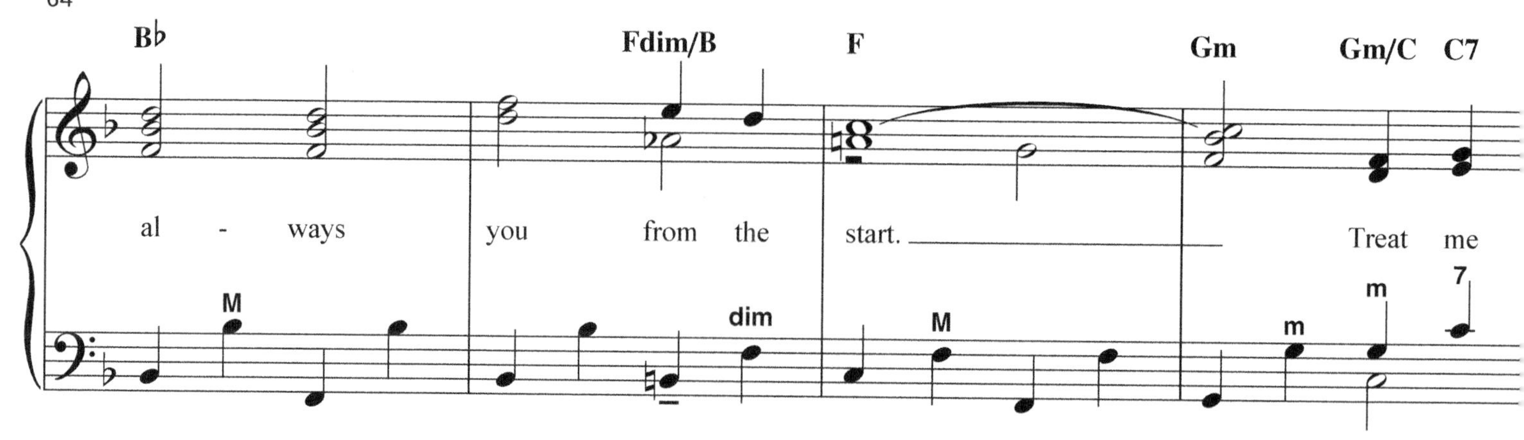
B♭
Fdim/B
F
Gm
Gm/C
C7
al - ways
you from the
start.
Treat me
M
dim
M
m
m
7

F
Gm
Am
Gm
F
nice, treat me
good, treat me
like you real - ly
should 'cause
M
m
m
m

D7
Gm
C7
I'm not made of
wood and I
don't have a
wood - en
7
m
7

1.
F
Gm
Gm/C
C7
2.
F
B♭
Am
Gm
F
3
heart.
Can't you
heart.
M
m
m
7
M
3